Forbush Memorial Library
118 MAIN STREET P.O. BOX 468
WESTMINSTER, MA 01473-0468

D1309377

DISCARD

CONTINENTS

ASIA

Forbush Memorial Library
118 MAIN STREET P.O. BOX 468
WESTMINSTER, MA 01473-0468

David Lambert

RSVP
RAINTREE
STECK-VAUGHN
PUBLISHERS
The Steck-Vaughn Company

Austin, Texas

CONTINENTS

AFRICA	EUROPE
ANTARCTICA	NORTH AMERICA
ASIA	SOUTH AMERICA

AUSTRALIA & OCEANIA

© Copyright 1998, text, Steck-Vaughn Company

All rights reserved. No part of this book may be reproduced or utilized in any form or by any means, electronic or mechanical, including photocopying, recording, or by any information storage and retrieval system, without permission in writing from the Publisher. Inquiries should be addressed to: Copyright Permissions, Steck-Vaughn Company, P.O. Box 26015, Austin, TX 78755.

Published by Raintree Steck-Vaughn Publishers, an imprint of Steck-Vaughn Company

Library of Congress Cataloging-in-Publication Data
Lambert, David.
Asia / David Lambert.
     p.   cm.—(Continents)
Includes bibliographical references and index.
Summary: Introduces the geography, history, peoples, industries, environment, and possible future of the largest continent in the world.
ISBN 0-8172-4781-5
1. Asia—Juvenile literature.
[X. Asia.]
X. Title. II. Series (Austin, Tex.)   Continents (series).
DS5.L35 1997
915—dc21   96-40278
     LAM

Printed in Italy. Bound in the United States.
1 2 3 4 5 6 7 8 9 0 01 00 99 98 97

Picture Acknowledgments
CM Dixon 18 top; Mary Evans Picture Library 22; Oxford Scientific Films 16 (Michael W Richards); Panos 12 top (Daniel O'Leary), 14 (Barbara Klass), 23 top (Jean-Leo Dugast), 31 bottom, 38 top (Chris Stowers), 40 bottom (Dominic Sansoni), 43 (Gangfeng Wang); Peter Newark's Pictures 23 bottom; Popperfoto 24, 25 (Patrick Baz), 27 (Jason Reed), 31 top (David Silverman); RGCP Pictures 17 bottom (Corel Corp), 37 (Corel Corp); Still Pictures 13 (Gil Moti), 21 Hartmut Schwarzbach), 28 (Mark Edwards), 29 (Hartmut Schwarzbach), 33 (Pierre Gleizes), 36, 41 (Gil Moti), 42 Mauri Rautkari); Tony Stone Images 8 (Earth Imaging), 9 (Paul Harris), 11 (Geoff Johnson), 12 bottom (World Perspectives), 15, 18 bottom (Alain le Garsmeur), 20 (Tom Till), 32 bottom (Yann Layma), 38 botto m (Ian Murphy); Trip 26 (Dinodia), 35.

All statistics on pages 4–7 come from *The World Almanac 1996*.

CONTENTS

ASIA BY COUNTRY

SOUTHWEST ASIA

Southwest Asia occupies less than one fifth of Asia, yet it holds 19 nations, or 20 counting the divided island of Cyprus as two. It also includes northeast Egypt. The largest country is Saudi Arabia, almost four times bigger than France. Oil wells have enriched the states facing the Persian Gulf, but much of the region consists of deserts and mountains where shepherds or farmers scratch a thin living. Most of Southwest Asia's people are Muslims. One of the main issues facing some of the countries in the region is Islamic fundamentalism. Muslims who support this growing movement wish to change their countries' laws and governments to reflect the teachings of the prophet Muhammad, as set out in the Islamic holy book, the Koran. This is causing conflict between the fundamentalists and the rulers of their nations.

YEMEN
Capital: Sanaa
Area: 205,356 sq. mi.
Population: 14,610,000
Currency: Rial
Average income($): 800
Principal language: Arabic
Principal religion: Muslim

OMAN
Capital: Muscat
Area: 118,150 sq. mi.
Population: 2,250,000
Currency: Rial
Average income ($): 5,600
Principal language: Arabic
Principal religion: Muslim

UNITED ARAB EMIRATES
Capital: Abu Dhabi
Area: 30,000 sq. mi.
Population: 2,900,000
Currency: Dirham
Average income ($): 22,500
Principal language: Arabic
Principal religion: Muslim

IRAQ
Capital: Baghdad
Area: 167,965 sq. mi.
Population: 20,600,000
Currency: Dinar
Average income ($): 2,000
Principal language: Arabic
Principal religion: Muslim

BAHRAIN
Capital: Manama
Area: 268 sq. mi.
Population: 575,900
Currency: Bahrain dinar
Average income ($): 7,900
Principal language: Arabic
Principal religion: Muslim

LEBANON
Capital: Beirut
Area: 3,950 sq. mi.
Population: 3,695,900
Currency: Lebanese pound
Average income ($): 1,750
Principal languages: Arabic, French
Principal religion: Muslim

IRAN
Capital: Tehran
Area: 632,457 sq. mi.
Population: 64,625,000
Currency: Rial
Average income ($): 4,750
Principal language: Persian
Principal religion: Muslim

AFGHANISTAN
Capital: Kabul
Area: 251,825 sq. mi.
Population: 21,251,800
Currency: Afghani
Average income($): 220
Principal languages: Pashtu, Dari
Principal religion: Muslim

GEORGIA
Capital: Tbilisi
Area: 26,900 sq. mi.
Population: 5,725,900
Currency: Coupon
Average income ($): 560
Principal language: Georgian
Principal religion: Christian

ARMENIA
Capital: Yerevan
Area: 11,500 sq. mi.
Population: 3,600,000
Currency: Dram
Average income ($): 660
Principal language: Armenian
Principal religion: Christian

AZERBAIJAN
Capital: Baku
Area: 33,400 sq. mi.
Population: 7,560,000
Currency: Manat
Average income ($): 730
Principal language: Azeri
Principal religion: Muslim

TURKEY
Capital: Ankara
Area: 300,948 sq. mi.
Population: 63,000,000
Currency: Lira
Average income ($): 2,100
Principal language: Turkish
Principal religion: Muslim

CYPRUS
Capital: Nicosia
Area: 3,572 sq. mi.
Population: 736,000
Currency: Cyprus pound
Average income ($): 8,640
Principal languages: Greek, Turkish
Principal religions: Christian, Muslim

SYRIA
Capital: Damascus
Area: 71,498 sq. mi.
Population: 15,451,900
Currency: Syrian pound
Average income ($): 1,250
Principal language: Arabic
Principal religion: Muslim

ISRAEL
Capital: Jerusalem
Area: 7,992 sq. mi.
Population: 5,700,000
Currency: Sheqel
Average income ($): 13,760
Principal languages: Hebrew, Arabic
Principal religions: Jewish, Muslim

QATAR
Capital: Doha
Area: 4,412 sq. mi.
Population: 534,000
Currency: Riyal
Average income ($): 15,150
Principal language: Arabic
Principal religion: Muslim

KUWAIT
Capital: Kuwait City
Area: 6,880 sq. mi.
Population: 1,817,000
Currency: Dinar
Average income ($): 23,350
Principal language: Arabic
Principal religion: Muslim

JORDAN
Capital: Amman
Area: 34,342 sq. mi.
Population: 4,100,700
Currency: Dinar
Average income ($): 1,200
Principal language: Arabic
Principal religion: Muslim

SAUDI ARABIA
Capital: Riyadh
Area: 865,000 sq. mi.
Population: 18,400,000
Currency: Riyal
Average income ($): 8,000
Principal language: Arabic
Principal religion: Muslim

Map labels:
BLACK SEA
Ankara
GEORGIA
TURKEY ARMENIA
Tbilisi
CYPRUS Nicosia
Yerevan AZERBAIJAN
Baku
LEBANON SYRIA
Beirut Damascus
CASPIAN SEA
Jerusalem
ISRAEL Amman
JORDAN Baghdad
IRAQ
Tehran
IRAN
AFGHANISTAN
Kabul
KUWAIT Kuwait City
PERSIAN GULF
Manama BAHRAIN
Riyadh QATAR
Doha
SAUDI ARABIA Abu Dhabi
RED SEA
UNITED ARAB EMIRATES
Muscat
Sana OMAN
YEMEN
ARABIAN SEA

0 200 400 600 800 km
0 100 200 300 500 600 miles

NORTH ASIA

North Asia consists of part of just one nation—the world's largest, Russia. More than half of Russia lies in North Asia, also called Siberia. This vast region of plains, plateaus, and mountains takes up more than one quarter of Asia; it is even bigger than Canada, the second largest country on Earth. Siberia is rich in minerals and timber, yet far fewer Russians live there than in European Russia. Long, bitter winters are one reason. When Russia was part of the Soviet Union its communist government controlled Siberia's mines and factories. Now people are free to build their own businesses, but a widening gap separates rich and poor.

RUSSIA
(Figures include Russia in Europe)
Capital: Moscow
Area: 6,592,800 sq. mi.
Population: 148,390,000
Currency: Ruble
Average income ($): 2,400
Principal language: Russian
Principal religion: Russian Orthodox

CENTRAL ASIA

Six nations lie entirely inside Central Asia, an area of grasslands, deserts, mountains, and an immense plateau. The six cover roughly one eighth of Asia, an area more than half the size of the United States, yet they hold fewer people than the United Kingdom. Until 1991, all but Mongolia formed part of the Soviet Union. The regions of Tibet and Xinjiang lie in Central Asia but they form part of the East Asian nation of China, so they do not appear with the countries listed on this page.

ARCTIC OCEAN

0   500   1000   1,500 km
0   250   500   750 miles

• Moscow

R U S S I A

Ural Mountains
(edge of Asia)

CASPIAN SEA

KAZAKHSTAN

ARAL SEA

TURKMENISTAN

UZBEKISTAN

Tashkent

• Alma-Ata

Ashkhabad

Bishkek

• Dushanbe

KYRGYZSTAN

TAJIKISTAN

Lake Balkhash

Lake Baikal

Ulan Bator •

MONGOLIA

SEA OF OKHOTSK

SEA OF JAPAN

TURKMENISTAN
Capital: Ashkhabad
Area: 188,500 sq. mi.
Population: 4,000,000
Currency: Manat
Average income ($): 1,400
Principal language: Turkmen
Principal religion: Muslim

KAZAKHSTAN
Capital: Alma-Ata
Area: 1,049,200 sq. mi.
Population: 17,300,000
Currency: Tenge
Average income ($): 1,540
Principal languages: Kazakh, Russian
Principal religions: Muslim, Christian

KYRGYZSTAN
Capital: Bishkek
Area: 76,600 sq. mi.
Population: 4,740,000
Currency: Som
Average income ($): 830
Principal languages: Kyrgyz, Russian
Principal religions: Muslim, Christian

UZBEKISTAN
Capital: Tashkent
Area: 172,700 sq. mi.
Population: 23,090,000
Currency: Som
Average income ($): 960
Principal language: Uzbek
Principal religion: Muslim

MONGOLIA
Capital: Ulan Bator
Area: 604,800 sq. mi.
Population: 2,410,000
Currency: Tugrik
Average income ($): 400
Principal language: Mongolian
Principal religion: Buddhist

TAJIKISTAN
Capital: Dushanbe
Area: 55,300 sq. mi.
Population: 6,100,000
Currency: Ruble
Average income ($): 470
Principal language: Tajik
Principal religion: Muslim

EAST ASIA

East Asia contains only five nations, yet they take up nearly one quarter of the whole continent—an area of productive plains and craggy mountain ranges, with volcanoes in Japan. By far the biggest nation is China, the world's third largest country. China occupies more than 90 percent of East Asia and holds the greatest population on Earth. China's and North Korea's communist governments largely control their citizens' lives, though China has begun to encourage people to run their own businesses. Free enterprise manufacturing and trade have made Japan, South Korea, and Taiwan East Asia's most prosperous nations.

NORTH KOREA
- Capital: Pyongyang
- Area: 47,399 sq. mi.
- Population: 23,930,000
- Currency: North Korean won
- Average income ($): 1,000
- Principal language: Korean
- Principal religion: Some Buddhism and Confucianism

SOUTH KOREA
- Capital: Seoul
- Area: 38,330 sq. mi.
- Population: 45,090,000
- Currency: South Korean won
- Average income ($): 7,670
- Principal language: Korean
- Principal religions: Christian, Buddhist

TAIWAN
- Capital: Taipei
- Area: 13,969 sq. mi.
- Population: 21,500,000
- Currency: New Taiwan dollar
- Average income ($): 11,000
- Principal languages: Mandarin Chinese
- Principal religions: Buddhist, Taoist, Confucian

JAPAN
- Capital: Tokyo
- Area: 145,850 sq. mi.
- Population: 125,160,000
- Currency: Yen
- Average income ($): 31,450
- Principal language: Japanese
- Principal religions: Shinto, Buddhist

CHINA
- Capital: Beijing
- Area: 3,696,100 sq. mi.
- Population: 1,203,097,000
- Currency: Yuan
- Average income ($): 370
- Principal language: Mandarin Chinese
- Principal religions: Officially none, but some Confucianism, Buddhism, Taoism

SOUTH ASIA

South Asia takes up only one tenth of Asia, but at least one third of all Asians live here, mostly on the hot, fertile plains and plateaus south of the world's highest peaks. There are seven countries, including the Maldives in the Indian Ocean, but India accounts for three quarters of all land and people. South Asia usually produces enough to feed its people but many are extremely poor.

INDIA
- Capital: New Delhi
- Area: 1,222,243 sq. mi.
- Population: 942,990,000
- Currency: Rupee
- Average income ($): 290
- Principal language: Hindi
- Principal religion: Hindu

NEPAL
- Capital: Katmandu
- Area: 56,827 sq. mi.
- Population: 21,950,000
- Currency: Nepalese rupee
- Average income ($): 160
- Principal language: Nepali
- Principal religion: Hindu

MALDIVES
- Capital: Malé
- Area: 115 sq.mi.
- Population: 261,000
- Currency: Rufiyaa
- Average income ($): 820
- Principal language: Divehi
- Principal religion: Muslim

BHUTAN
- Capital: Thimpu
- Area: 18,150 sq. mi.
- Population: 1,700,000
- Currency: Ngultrum
- Average income ($): 180
- Principal language: Dzongkha (official)
- Principal religion: Buddhist

SRI LANKA
- Capital: Colombo
- Area: 25,332 sq. mi.
- Population: 18,360,000
- Currency: Rupee
- Average income ($): 600
- Principal language: Sinhala
- Principal religion: Buddhist

BANGLADESH
- Capital: Dhaka
- Area: 57,925 sq. mi.
- Population: 128,340,000
- Currency: Taka
- Average income ($): 220
- Principal language: Bengla (official)
- Principal religion: Muslim

PAKISTAN
- Capital: Islamabad
- Area: 339,697 sq. mi.
- Population: 131,500,000
- Currency: Rupee
- Average income ($): 430
- Principal languages: Urdu, English (both official)
- Principal religion: Muslim

SEA OF JAPAN

NORTH KOREA
JAPAN
Pyongyang
Seoul
Tokyo
SOUTH KOREA

Beijing

C H I N A

EAST CHINA SEA
PACIFIC OCEAN

Islamabad

PAKISTAN

New Delhi
NEPAL
Katmandu
BHUTAN
Thimpu
Dhaka

ARABIAN SEA

I N D I A

Taipei
TAIWAN

SOUTH CHINA SEA

0   500   1,000 km
0 200 400 600 miles

BANGLADESH

BAY OF BENGAL

SRI LANKA
Colombo
Malé
MALDIVES

SOUTHEAST ASIA

Ten countries occupy the peninsulas and islands that form this warm, moist corner of Asia, with lush lowlands and forested volcanoes and other mountains. Only about 10 percent of Asia lies in this region, but two of its countries—Indonesia and the Philippines—include thousands of islands. There are rich resources of soil, forests, and minerals, and some Southeast Asian cities are growing prosperous from manufacturing and trade. But as people's numbers and needs multiply, overuse of land becomes a problem.

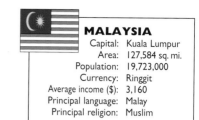

MALAYSIA
Capital: Kuala Lumpur
Area: 127,584 sq. mi.
Population: 19,723,000
Currency: Ringgit
Average income ($): 3,160
Principal language: Malay
Principal religion: Muslim

MYANMAR (BURMA)
Capital: Rangoon
Area: 261,228 sq. mi.
Population: 43,500,000
Currency: Kyat
Average income ($): 500
Principal language: Burmese
Principal religion: Buddhist

THAILAND
Capital: Bangkok
Area: 198,115 sq. mi.
Population: 60,271,000
Currency: Baht
Average income ($): 2,040
Principal language: Thai
Principal religion: Buddhist

VIETNAM
Capital: Hanoi
Area: 127,246 sq. mi.
Population: 74,580,000
Currency: Dong
Average income ($): 170
Principal language: Vietnamese
Principal religion: Buddhist

BRUNEI
Capital: Bandar Seri Begawan
Area: 2,239 sq. mi.
Population: 292,000
Currency: Brunei dollar
Average income ($): 6,000
Principal language: Malay
Principal religion: Muslim

PHILIPPINES
Capital: Manila
Area: 115,860 sq. mi.
Population: 73,266,000
Currency: Peso
Average income ($): 830
Principal languages: Filipino, English
Principal religion: Christian

LAOS
Capital: Vientiane
Area: 91,429 sq. mi.
Population: 4,910,000
Currency: New Kip
Average income ($): 290
Principal language: Laotian
Principal religion: Buddhist

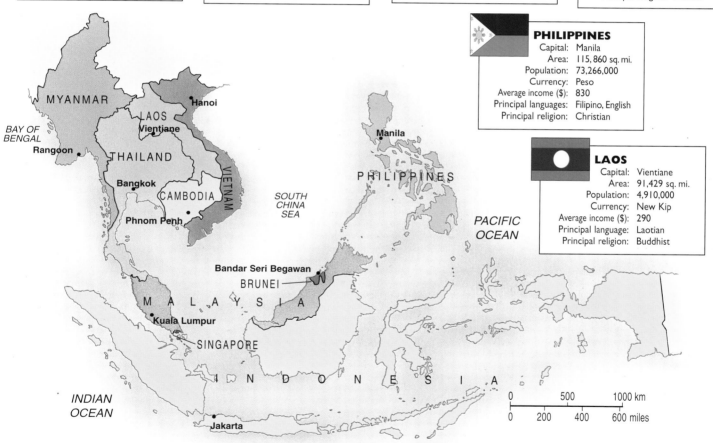

BAY OF BENGAL

MYANMAR

LAOS
• Hanoi
Vientiane •

Rangoon •

THAILAND

Bangkok •

CAMBODIA

Phnom Penh •

VIETNAM

SOUTH CHINA SEA

Manila •

PHILIPPINES

PACIFIC OCEAN

Bandar Seri Begawan •
BRUNEI

M A L A Y S I A

Kuala Lumpur •

SINGAPORE

I N D O N E S I A

INDIAN OCEAN

Jakarta •

| 0 | 500 | 1000 km |
| 0 | 200 | 400 | 600 miles |

SINGAPORE
Capital: Singapore
Area: 247 sq. mi.
Population: 2,990,000
Currency: Singapore dollar
Average income ($): 19,310
Principal language: Chinese (Malay, Tamil, and English also are official)
Principal religion: Buddhist

INDONESIA
Capital: Jakarta
Area: 741,052 sq. mi.
Population: 203,583,000
Currency: Rupiah
Average income ($): 730
Principal language: Bahasa Indonesia (Malay)
Principal religion: Muslim

CAMBODIA
Capital: Phnom Penh
Area: 70,238 sq. mi.
Population: 10,561,000
Currency: Riel
Average income ($): 200
Principal language: Khmer
Principal religion: Buddhist

INTRODUCTION

If all the land on Earth formed one great pie and you cut off a third of it, that slice would be the size of Asia, the largest continent of all. Asia is more than four times bigger than Europe to its west and nearly twice as big as North America beyond the Pacific Ocean to its east. Not surprisingly, this vast continent has a great diversity of physical features, climates, and wildlife.

Imagine flying across northern Asia from the Ural Mountains, where Asia and Europe meet, to the narrow Bering Strait where Asia almost touches North America. If you follow the imaginary Arctic Circle, all you see below are boggy plains, dark forests, great snaking rivers, and cold mountain ranges. Your journey takes you one third of the way around the Northern Hemisphere and through nine time zones. If you reach Asia's eastern end at midnight, it will still be afternoon where you began.

Asia is immense from north to south as well. From the Arctic Ocean's icy shores to the Indian Ocean's palm-fringed beaches is nearly one quarter of the way around the Earth. This journey would take you from northern Russia's cold Arctic plains and mountain forests to the empty Gobi Desert of Mongolia. Then you would fly on past the Tibetan Plateau's high, rugged eastern rim to the hot, humid rice fields and forests, teeming cities, and old temples of tropical Malaysia and Indonesia.

Below Asia lies to the west of the Pacific Ocean as shown in this photograph taken from a satellite orbiting the Earth.

Right This world map shows Asia's size compared with that of North and South America, Europe, Africa, and Australasia. Huge peninsulas jut out to the south and east, but Asia's northern shore is much straighter.

ASIA'S SPECIAL FEATURES

Much in Asia is unique. Arabia in Southwest Asia is the world's largest peninsula. One place in Central Asia stands farther from the sea than any other spot on Earth. Between Nepal and China towers Earth's highest peak, Mt. Everest. Where Israel and Jordan meet lies our planet's lowest land, the Dead Sea shore. Lake Baikal in eastern Russia is the deepest lake, and north of Iran extends the largest lake, the Caspian Sea, an inland stretch of water bigger than Germany.

Asia holds weather records, too. The greatest temperature difference between winter and summer occurs in eastern Russia, and Cherrapunji, a mountain village in India, holds the all-time record for the most rain in a year.

Asia's peoples are equally remarkable. Thousands of years ago they made inventions and discoveries that all of us depend upon today. Many of the foods we eat come from plants and animals first farmed or tamed in Asia. It was there that people first learned to build and live in villages, towns, and cities. Asians invented boats, wheels, writing, money, paper, and gunpowder. They also founded all the world's great religions.

Today the world's biggest country, Russia, sprawls all the way across Asia, and no other continent contains so many people, with scores of groups and languages. Millions of Asian peasants are among the poorest humans anywhere, but where new factories spring up, Asian businessmen are fast becoming millionaires.

Above His fur hood helps keep this reindeer herder warm in eastern Russia, where winters are among the coldest anywhere outside Antarctica.

THE GEOGRAPHY OF ASIA

Asia grew piece by piece, rather like a logjam. Its main "logs" were great rocky slabs, or plates, floating on the mantle—the layer of semimolten rock below the earth's outer crust. These plates were mini-continents, but between them were stringy mountainous islands.

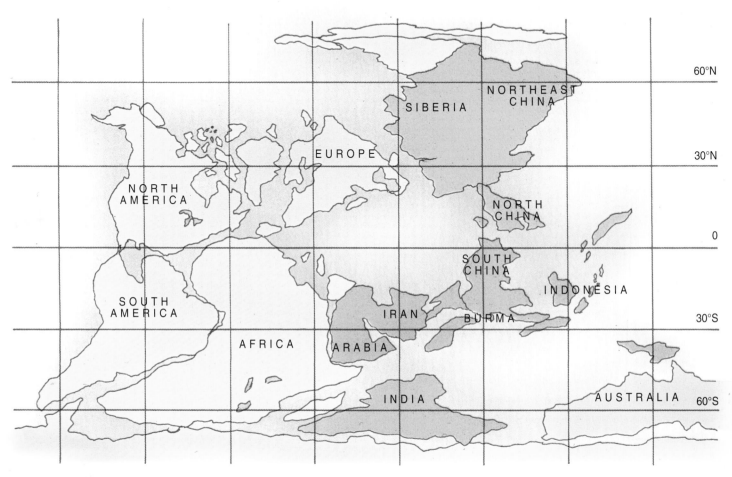

MOUNTAINS, PLAINS, AND DESERTS

Over the last 500 million years, plates drifting north have collided and stuck together. The oldest mini-continent was Angara, now part of Siberia. Where plates and islands were pushed up against Siberia or one another, their slowly crashing edges pushed up volcanic rocks and seafloor sediments into long, snaky mountain ranges. The Altai Mountains, and others now found deep in Central Asia, were formed in that way. The Ural Mountains rose where Europe and Asia met. The Himalayas, the world's highest peaks, sprang up where the giant island of India began colliding with Asia about 50 million years ago. North of the Himalayas, the same slow crash forced up a mighty tableland, the Tibetan Plateau, the largest mountain region on Earth. East Asia and mainland Southeast Asia had already latched onto the continent. Later a great crack in the earth's crust separated Africa from Arabia, which swung north and became the Arabian Peninsula of Southwest Asia.

The world might have looked like this 300 million years ago. Small bits of land had not yet joined to form the mighty continent of Asia.

The great belt of mountains now crossing Asia from Turkey to China is largely made of old seafloor sediments pushed up, as plates drifting north squeezed an ancient sea out of existence.

Meanwhile, groups of islands grew off East and Southeast Asia. There the fronts of heavy oceanic plates slid down under Asia, bearing lighter sediments on their backs. Far below, heat melted the lighter rocks. These then burned holes through the solid oceanic crust and burst up as rows of volcanoes. Such fiery mountains helped build Japan, the Kuril Islands, the Philippines, and parts of Indonesia.

As Asia's mountains rose, weather worked to wear them down. Frost, glaciers, and rivers cut deep, narrow valleys in the high, young Himalayas and smoothed ancient uplands into hills or plains. Much of the Arabian Peninsula is now a low desert called the Rub al Khali, and western North Asia has the low West Siberian Plain, with the Turanian Plain of Central Asia to its south. On Asia's lowlands, great rivers dump ground-up scraps of rock that they have washed down from the mountains. At river mouths all this sand, silt, and mud builds lowlands out into the sea.

Sharp peaks soar above deep valleys in the Himalaya mountains of Nepal.

"LIKE AN ATOMIC BOMB EXPLODING"

Asia's Pacific Rim forms part of the so-called Ring of Fire circling the Pacific Ocean. Eruptions and earthquakes often shake its coasts and islands. Indonesia alone has more active volcanoes than anywhere else on Earth, and the 20th century's third biggest eruption happened in the Philippines. In 1991 Mt. Pinatubo hurled a cloud of scalding ash 19 miles high. Rain turned the ash to mud and swallowed up 200,000 homes. A million farm animals and 700 people died. One survivor said, "It looked like an atomic bomb exploding. Small rocks rained from the sky. To save ourselves we jammed cardboard boxes on our heads with peepholes for our eyes. Then we tried to run away, but the roads were slippery with mud. One mudflow crushed my home and killed a whole year's crops."

RIVERS, LAKES, AND SEAS

Major rivers cross most parts of Asia. Four of the longest rivers pass through North Asia. The Lena, Ob, and Yenisey flow north across Russia to the Arctic Ocean, while the Amur River heads east between Russia and China toward the Pacific.

The Tigris and Euphrates are the two biggest rivers in Southwest Asia. Both run from Turkey through Iraq and then meet and flow into the Persian Gulf. The famous Jordan River is a smaller stream that flows from Lebanon between Israel and Jordan to one of the world's saltiest lakes, the Dead Sea. The Jordan shrinks as it goes, because pipes carry off water for thirsty farm crops.

Three great rivers run through South Asia from the Himalayas in the north. The Indus crosses Pakistan to the Arabian Sea. The Brahmaputra and Ganges cross northern India and Bangladesh and empty into the Bay of Bengal. All three carry massive loads of mud and silt, largely scraps of rock worn off the vast Tibetan Plateau. Tibet supplies 25 percent of all sediment that rivers wash into the world's seas. The Ganges and Brahmaputra have dumped enough sediment to build an apron of lowland far out into the Bay of Bengal. This apron forms the world's largest delta.

Above The Euphrates River water flows through an irrigation ditch to moisten crops growing in a field in Syria.

From Tibet or nearby mountains, the Irrawaddy, Salween, Chao Phraya, and Mekong—four great rivers of Southeast Asia—flow south to the sea.

The Yangtze and Huang Ho (Yellow River) also rise in Tibet. The Yangtze is arguably the longest river in Asia. Both these major East Asian rivers flow east through China to seas that fringe the Pacific.

In Central Asia, the Amu Darya and Syr Darya feed into the landlocked Aral Sea, but many of this region's rivers dry up crossing deserts.

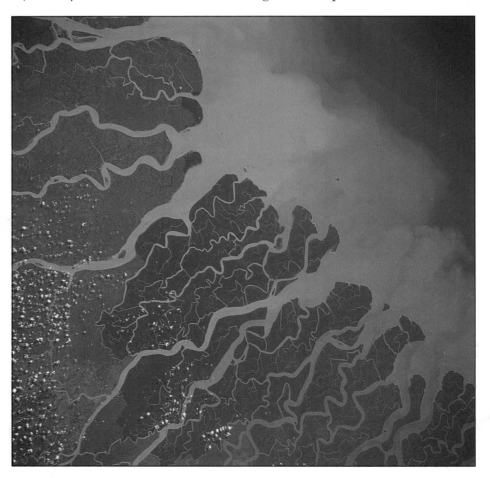

Left Pale sediment pours into the Bay of Bengal from streams that flow across the Ganges-Brahmaputra Delta. Seen from high above, the streams look like wriggly tentacles.

The continent's largest lakes include the Caspian Sea and Aral Sea in Central Asia, and lakes Baikal and Balkhash in Asian Russia. Lake Baikal holds 20 percent of all the fresh water on Earth, but the others are salty.

Some rivers flow into lakes, but Asia's biggest natural waterways end in the sea. Sea surrounds most of the continent. To the north lies the cold Arctic Ocean, frozen for much of the year. To the east lie seas that fringe the Pacific Ocean. To the south are the warm Arabian Sea and Bay of Bengal, parts of the Indian Ocean. In the Southwest the Black Sea is linked to the Mediterranean Sea, an arm of the Atlantic Ocean.

Asia's coast is so long that if you could straighten it out, it would stretch three times around the equator.

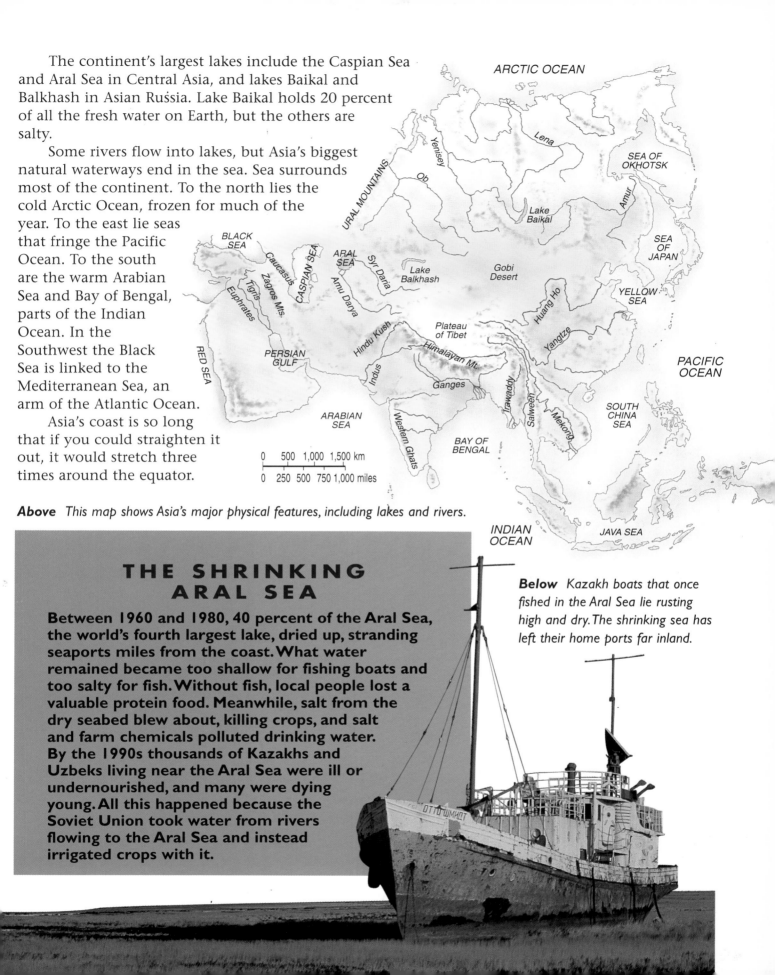

Above This map shows Asia's major physical features, including lakes and rivers.

THE SHRINKING ARAL SEA

Between 1960 and 1980, 40 percent of the Aral Sea, the world's fourth largest lake, dried up, stranding seaports miles from the coast. What water remained became too shallow for fishing boats and too salty for fish. Without fish, local people lost a valuable protein food. Meanwhile, salt from the dry seabed blew about, killing crops, and salt and farm chemicals polluted drinking water. By the 1990s thousands of Kazakhs and Uzbeks living near the Aral Sea were ill or undernourished, and many were dying young. All this happened because the Soviet Union took water from rivers flowing to the Aral Sea and instead irrigated crops with it.

Below Kazakh boats that once fished in the Aral Sea lie rusting high and dry. The shrinking sea has left their home ports far inland.

CLIMATE AND WEATHER

Asia has eight main types of climate.

• North Asia's Arctic coast and the continent's highest mountains have a polar climate, always cold and usually dry.

• South of the Arctic coast, much of North Asia and the Tibetan Plateau have subarctic conditions. Summers there are brief and cool, while winters are long and very cold. Most of the year's light rain or snow falls in summer.

• Southwestern parts of North Asia, Central Asia, and East Asia (northeast China, the Koreas, and northern Japan) have a moist continental climate. Winters are cold and summers are warm. There is some rain in summer and some snow in winter.

• East Mediterranean countries, Iraq, and northwest Iran have hot, dry summers and mild winters with some rain—sometimes called a Mediterranean climate.

• Between the southern Black Sea and Caspian Sea, and in southern China and Japan, summers are warm or hot, winters are cool or mild, and some rain falls at all times of the year. These regions have a moist subtropical climate.

• A great belt of land with an arid to semiarid climate stretches across Southwest and much of Central Asia. It is almost always dry there. Some places become much hotter than others in summer, but everywhere nights are much cooler than days.

• Most of South and mainland Southeast Asia have a tropical wet and dry climate. It is always hot, with a rainy season and a dry season.

• The islands and coasts of Southeast Asia experience a tropical rainy climate: hot with plenty of rain all the year.

WHEN CYCLONES STRIKE

Sometimes severe storms called cyclones drive seawater north through the Bay of Bengal. A wall of seawater can sweep across the low, coastal islands of Bangladesh, swamping villages and drowning hundreds of thousands of people. One survivor of the floods of 1991 said, "I managed to climb a palm tree and hang on for hours. The sea kept rising and the fierce wind nearly tore me off. When the water went down many of my friends and relatives had drowned. Sea salt had ruined our rice crop and got into our drinking water. This is my home so I must stay here, but I know it could happen again."

Boats sail on a huge floodwater lake in a low-lying part of Bangladesh. Drowned crops rot in underwater fields.

Above Winter snow cloaks Mount Fuji, but in Japan summer is the wettest time of year.

MONSOONS

In much of Asia, rainfall depends on seasonal winds called monsoons. Monsoon winds reverse their direction at different times of year. In the summer hot air rises and thins out above the warm Asian landmass. To take its place, air flows in from the sea, and moist winds bring heavy rain to much of South, Southeast, and East Asia. But in the winter, dense, cold, air sinks over the chilly Asian landmass. Dry winds blow out from the middle. Then much of South, Southeast, and East Asia receive little or no rain.

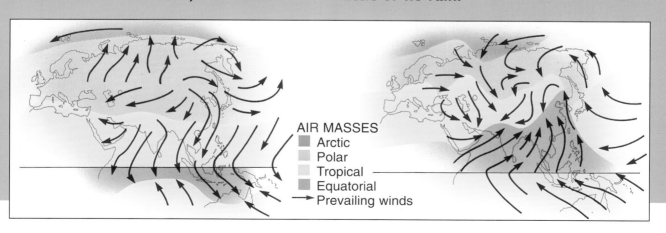

AIR MASSES
- Arctic
- Polar
- Tropical
- Equatorial
→ Prevailing winds

Above In January dry winds blow out of Central Asia to surrounding lands.

Above In July moist winds blow into Asia from the seas around its rim.

PLANTS AND WILDLIFE

Asia's wild plants and animals vary from place to place, for each kind needs a special set of conditions—a particular type of climate, for instance. Except in the coldest and driest lands, though, most natural vegetation and wildlife have given way to farm crops and animals.

Only the hardiest plants can survive Asia's coldest places. Ground-hugging plants shaped like little cushions brave the bitter winds that scour high mountains. Up there vultures soar and mountain goats leap nimbly from crag to crag.

In the far north, grasses, mosses, and flowering plants grow in the brief summers of the cold, boggy, and stony lowlands known as the tundra or "treeless plain." Tree roots cannot penetrate its permafrost, the ever-frozen soil below the surface. Wolves hunt reindeer and, in winter, polar bears wander onto the frozen sea to catch seals rising to breathe at holes in the ice.

South of the tundra, a vast belt of coniferous forest called taiga crosses North Asia. Its trees include larches and evergreen pines, firs, and spruces. Tough narrow leaves and springy branches help these trees survive cold winters and heavy loads of snow. The taiga is home to brown bears, lynxes, wolverines, and squirrels.

South of the taiga, a belt of treeless grassland called the steppe once covered southwestern Siberia, though much has been plowed up and farmed. Where grassland remains, saiga antelopes roam the plains, and steppe eagles swoop on burrowing ground squirrels called susliks.

South of the steppe, plants that need little moisture survive in the deserts and semideserts that sprawl from Arabia across much of Central Asia. Clumps of grass and low shrubby plants sprout here and there among bare sand and rock, and bushy acacias or tamarisks line dry riverbeds. Wild camels once lived in these deserts. Lizards, tortoises, gazelles, and small jumping rodents called jerboas still do.

Near the Mediterranean Sea, tough shiny leaves that store moisture help evergreen shrubs and broadleafed trees survive long, hot summers. In northern East Asia, where winters are colder, broadleaf forest trees survive the winter by shedding their leaves.

Low-growing plants flower in the brief Arctic summer on Wrangel Island, in northern Russia. Icebergs drifting offshore pose a danger to ships.

Leaf shedding also helps teak and other broadleaf trees of the deciduous tropical forests of South and Southeast Asia. Leafless trees lose little moisture through the long, hot dry season. In open areas, tall tropical grasses can conceal tigers, Asian elephants, and other large mammals.

Evergreen tropical rain forest thrives in the hot, rainy lowlands of Southeast Asia. Giant trees with pillarlike trunks and broad, pointed leaves soar above the rest of the forest. Its floor is open enough to walk across except where people have cut down the trees. Then a dense jungle of shrubs and small trees springs up. The orangutan and Sumatran rhinoceros are among the rare creatures found in some of these forests.

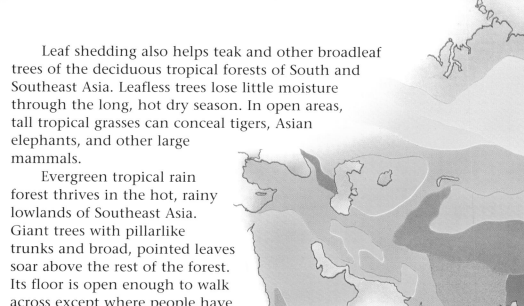

VEGETATION ZONES

- Tundra
- Taiga
- Temperate forest
- Steppe and dry grassland
- Mountain
- Tropical savanna
- Tropical rain forest
- Hot desert

Above This map shows the main types of natural vegetation found in Asia.

TIGERS

The largest, palest tigers are the Siberian tigers of northeast Asia. Their large size and long coats help them store body heat in the cold winters there. Much farther south, the smallest, darkest tigers lived in the hot tropical forests of the Indonesian island of Bali. Asia had about 100,000 tigers in 1900, but fewer than 7,000 still survive. The Bali, Caspian, and Javan tigers have become extinct. Siberian tigers are scarce, and the commonest kind—the Bengal tiger of the Indian subcontinent—is far less common than it used to be.

Below A Bengal tiger lies half submerged in a forest pool in India. At the hottest time of year, tigers like to stand or lie in water to keep cool or rest in deep shade under trees or cliffs.

THE HISTORY OF ASIA

The first Asians were Old Stone Age hunter-gatherers who probably arrived from Africa about two million years ago. Humans like ourselves appeared much later. By 100,000 years ago some lived where Israel stands today, but they still used stone and wooden tools and weapons and depended on wild plants and animals for food.

THE FIRST CIVILIZATION

By 10,000 years ago, though, Southwest Asian peoples were making an astonishing discovery: By growing wheat and taming goats and cattle, they gained a surer food supply than just by gathering and hunting. Farming and stock raising marked the beginning of the New Stone Age. To tend their crops, New Stone Age farmers had to settle down. Their clustered homes became the world's first villages and towns. More food meant fewer humans starved to death, so people multiplied. Where rivers watered fertile land, farming villages and towns sprang up through Asia from Turkey to China.

Above *Sumerians lead cattle, sheep, and goats and carry sacks of grain in this picture made of shells and colored bits of stone stuck in bitumen. This so-called Standard of Ur was made 4,500 years ago and was dug up from an old tomb in Iraq.*

Fresh discoveries and inventions helped the Sumerians in what is now Iraq to build the world's first civilization. By 5,000 years ago Sumerians had oxen pulling plows, wheeled carts, irrigated fields, bronze weapons, sailing ships, and writing. In Mesopotamia (the land between the Tigris and Euphrates rivers) farmers produced enough spare food for carpenters, potters, and other full-time craftspeople making tools the farmers needed. Sumeria's Bronze Age towns grew into cities controlling the land around and trading food and manufactured goods for copper, tin, stone, and timber brought from faraway places.

Right *Chinese soldiers stroll along the Great Wall of China. Built more than 2,000 years ago to keep out China's northern enemies, the wall was later extended to nearly 3,980 miles long. In time much of it fell down but parts have been rebuilt.*

CITY-STATES AND EMPIRES

Priests or kings ruled the city-states that sprang up in Mesopotamia, the Indus Valley (in what is now Pakistan), and north and central China. They built great temples, tombs, palaces, defensive walls, and irrigation canals. But rivalry among city-states sparked off wars and conquests. Strong city-states seized their weaker neighbors, creating early nations such as Assyria and Babylonia in Mesopotamia. As iron grew cheap and plentiful, by 500 B.C. iron spearheads and arrowheads were helping some nations' armies crush others, winning empires. Three of the greatest early Iron Age empires were those of Persia, India, and China.

Asia's empires grew from the croplands of the plains and river valleys around the continent's rim. But these rich farmlands offered tempting targets to the poor herdsmen and shepherds in the deserts and dry grasslands of Central Asia and Arabia.

From time to time hordes of mounted archers swarmed out of Central Asia. The so-called Aryans probably destroyed the Bronze Age Indus Valley cities. By 214 B.C. the first Chinese emperor had built the Great Wall of China to keep out nomadic tribes, but by A.D. 500 the Huns of Mongolia had invaded northern China, India, and Europe—where they helped destroy the West Roman Empire. By the 1500s Mongols had overrun Persia, China, and India, and the Ottoman Turks held much of Southwest Asia. Meanwhile, in the seventh century A.D., Muslim armies from Arabia had won an Arab Empire that briefly stretched from Portugal to India.

UNEARTHING AN ANCIENT ARMY

In 1974 Chinese villagers dug a well for water but found something much more exciting: a whole army of life-size baked-clay model soldiers 2,200 years old. Archaeologists unearthed 8,000 figures altogether. There were foot soldiers with spears and swords, archers with bows and arrows, and charioteers, together with their horses. Many people suppose that the model army's task was to protect the tomb of the first Chinese emperor, Qin Shi Huang-di.

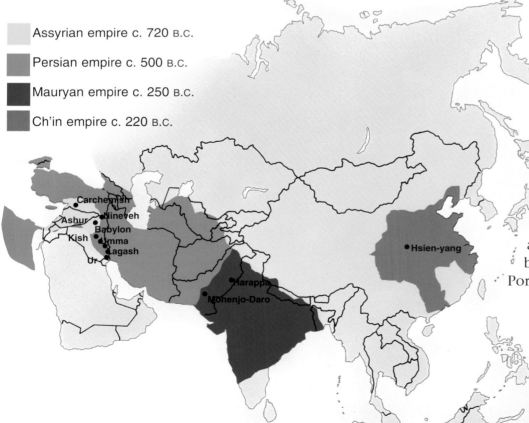

Assyrian empire c. 720 B.C.

Persian empire c. 500 B.C.

Mauryan empire c. 250 B.C.

Ch'in empire c. 220 B.C.

Asia has been home to many great civilizations, from the Sumerians in the west to the Chinese in the east.

ASIA'S IMPACT ON THE WORLD

Long ago, Asian peoples began affecting other continents. Asia was the springboard from which humans peopled Australia, the Americas, and Pacific islands. From Southeast Asia, Old Stone Age hunter-gatherers reached Australia by 60,000 years ago. From Siberia, hunter-gatherers reached Alaska, and about 10,000 years ago their descendants populated the Americas. By A.D. 1000, New Stone Age farmers sailing in canoes from Southeast Asia had colonized Pacific islands from Hawaii to New Zealand. Heading west across the Indian Ocean, Southeast Asian farmers also settled Madagascar.

From Southwest Asia, farming, city building, writing, money, and more ingredients of civilization spread to Europe by 2,500 years ago. By the second century B.C., trade linked Asia's civilizations with one another and with Europe. Camels carried precious silks along the Silk Road running through Central Asia's steppes and deserts from China to the East Mediterranean. In Roman times, sailing ships blown along by monsoon winds were already crossing the Indian Ocean to connect East Asia with North Africa and Europe.

New Asian food plants, including apricot and peach trees, rice, and sugarcane reached southern Europe after about A.D. 700 with the Arabs, who conquered North Africa and Spain. From the Arabs, Europeans also learned of the Chinese inventions gunpowder and paper and the Indian way of writing numbers that we use today.

Giant stone statues stand on Easter Island west of South America. Their makers were Polynesians—a people who came from Asia to remote Pacific islands long before European explorers arrived.

THE BIRTHPLACE OF RELIGIONS

Asians not only made important inventions and discoveries, but also started all the world's great religions: Hinduism, Buddhism, Judaism, Christianity, and Islam. Hinduism developed in India perhaps 4,000 years ago. Hindus believe in many gods and think dead people's souls live on in humans or animals.

Siddhartha Gautama—also called the Buddha—founded Buddhism in India more than 2,500 years ago. The religion then spread to China, Japan, and Thailand.

Judaism is the ancient faith of the Jews of Palestine, now held by Jews worldwide. Judaism claims there is one God and the Hebrew Bible holds his teachings. The Jewish preacher Jesus (also called Christ) added new teachings and founded Christianity in Palestine nearly 2,000 years ago. Christians believe in Jesus as God's son. Christianity is now the chief religion in North Asia, Europe, southern Africa, the Americas, and Australasia.

The Arab prophet Muhammad preached Islam in Arabia nearly 1,400 years ago. Muhammad's followers, called Muslims, believe in one God and say the Koran contains his teachings. Islam is strongest in Southwest, South, and Southeast Asia and in northern Africa.

In one way or another, then, the entire world owes much to Asia's peoples and their discoveries, inventions, and beliefs.

Below Muslims in an Indian mosque face toward Mecca, their holy city in far-off Saudi Arabia, while they kneel for midday prayers. About 100 million Muslims live in India, about one for every ten Hindus.

Right This world map shows where various religious faiths are strongest. Islam, Hinduism, Buddhism, Christianity, and Judaism are all important in one part of Asia or another, and so are Chinese and Japanese religions, which include Taoism, Confucianism, and Shintoism.

Christianity

Local religions

Islam

Hinduism

Buddhism

Chinese and Japanese religions

Judaism

None

EARLY WESTERN INFLUENCE

Early on in European history, several European powers tried to stamp their mark on Southwest Asia. In 334 B.C., Alexander the Great led a Greek army east through Southwest Asia. In 12 years he crushed the Persian Empire and won a so-called Hellenistic Empire that sprawled from Greece to India. Alexander's empire soon broke up into three kingdoms, but Greek became an everyday language in the eastern Mediterranean, Greek art styles reached India, and trade linked Greece with China.

About A.D. 100, the Romans of Italy seized much of Southwest Asia. By then the Roman Empire stretched from Portugal to the Persian Gulf, and Roman merchants traded with regions much farther east. We know this from gold Roman coins that have been found in southern India and Southeast Asia.

This medieval miniature painting depicts Christian knights preparing to sail on a crusade against Muslims in the east Mediterranean.

WARS OF RELIGION

The East Roman, or Byzantine, Empire hung on to part of Southwest Asia long after the West Roman Empire based in Italy collapsed. But by A.D. 700 the Byzantines had lost the Christians' holy land of Palestine to Arab Muslims. Winning back Palestine from its Muslim rulers became the reason for a fresh European attack on Southwest Asia. In A.D. 1098 an army of West European knights launched the First Crusade against Syria and Palestine. More crusades followed, but the Christians lost the lands they had gained and the Muslims finally forced them out in 1291. The Crusades, which occupied much of Europe's ruling class for almost 200 years, had been little more than a fleabite on Asia's southwestern flank.

CONQUEST AND TRADE

By 1500 Europeans had begun to make a far longer-lasting, deeper, and more widespread impact on Asia. First, Portuguese ships reached India and China, seeking spices and other Asian luxuries. By 1700, Spanish, Dutch, and English ships had joined in this profitable Eastern trade. Largely to protect their Asian trade from one another, the Europeans sent troops and set up colonies in India, Southeast Asia, and China.

By the 19th century, the new factory towns of the Industrial Revolution gave Europeans and Americans better weapons and tools than those of Asian countries. The West's Industrial Revolution had also given it prosperity and a growing taste for Asian products such as tea, silk, porcelain and, later, rubber. So the West's hold tightened on the East. By 1900 Russia held North Asia and west Central Asia; the British held South Asia; and Great Britain, the Netherlands, France, and the United States ruled different parts of Southeast Asia.

Above *One of Calcutta's most impressive buildings is the Victoria Memorial, built by the British when India was part of Great Britain's colonial empire.*

European traders and estate owners paid low wages to their Asian workers, but Western colonial powers brought benefits as well. They introduced such things as public health programs, railroads, Western ideas of law and government, impressive buildings, and three valuable food crops: corn, peanuts, and sweet potatoes.

Left *Old drawings show British tea planters using Indians to roll tea leaves, weigh and pack tea, and take it to be shipped from India to Great Britain.*

A CENTURY OF CHANGE

In 1900, Asian countries were mostly poor, technologically backward, and run by Western powers. As the 20th century reached its end, almost all ruled themselves, and modern factories and cities were making some of them among the richest nations on Earth.

Japan had begun modernizing even before 1900. In 1904 the powerful Japanese navy sank a Russian fleet and showed the world that Western countries were not unbeatable. In the 1930s Japanese troops invaded Manchuria, part of China. In the early 1940s, during World War II, Japan seized much of East and Southeast Asia from the Western powers until pushed back by U.S. and Allied forces. Only in 1945, after U.S. atom bombs had flattened the Japanese cities of Hiroshima and Nagasaki, did Japan surrender.

Below *After the Bolshevik Revolution of 1917, Russia and the countries ruled by Russia came under communist control.*

INDEPENDENCE AND CONFLICT

After World War II, Western powers took back their Asian territories, but not for long. Dissatisfied with rule by foreigners, Asian peoples began to demand—and achieve—independence. By 1949 new Asian nations included what are now Israel, Jordan, Lebanon, Syria, Kuwait, Pakistan, India, Sri Lanka, Myanmar, Laos, Indonesia, the Philippines, and North and South Korea. Much of the rest of Southwest, South, and Southeast Asia was independent by 1971. Apart from Mongolia, Central Asia's nations emerged only after the Soviet Union broke up in 1991.

Before then, the communist Soviet Union and communist China had become the two great Asian powers, with much influence across the continent. When wars between communists and non-communists flared up in smaller Asian countries, China and the Soviet Union helped the communist side while the United States and its allies backed the non-communists. The worst conflicts were the Korean War (1950–53) and the Vietnam War (1957–75).

Below *This map shows when Asian countries gained their freedom from the Western powers that governed them.*

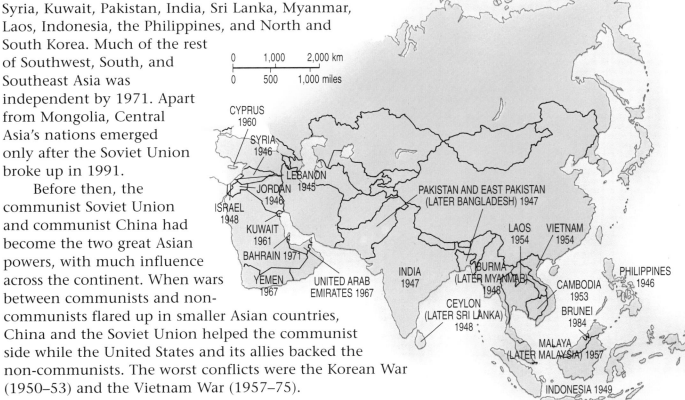

CYPRUS 1960
SYRIA 1946
LEBANON 1945
JORDAN 1946
ISRAEL 1948
KUWAIT 1961
BAHRAIN 1971
YEMEN 1967
UNITED ARAB EMIRATES 1967
PAKISTAN AND EAST PAKISTAN (LATER BANGLADESH) 1947
INDIA 1947
CEYLON (LATER SRI LANKA) 1948
BURMA (LATER MYANMAR) 1948
LAOS 1954
VIETNAM 1954
CAMBODIA 1953
BRUNEI 1984
MALAYA (LATER MALAYSIA) 1957
PHILIPPINES 1946
INDONESIA 1949

0   1,000   2,000 km
0   500   1,000 miles

At the western end of Asia, Jews and Arabs have been at odds since 1948, when the United Nations formed the Jewish nation of Israel out of part of what had been the chiefly Muslim state of Palestine. Nearby Arab countries attacked Israel several times but failed to destroy it.

Elsewhere in Southwest Asia, Afghanistan began a long civil war in 1978, and in 1990 Iraq invaded its small but oil-rich neighbor, Kuwait. The following year, U.S. and allied troops drove out the Iraqis.

Palestinian Arabs hurl stones at police in Gaza City, seized by Israel from Egypt in 1967. Poor and numerous, Gaza's Arabs have often clashed with Israel's Jewish government.

TIGERS AND LITTLE TIGERS

Despite such wars, by the end of the 20th century, oil and manufacturing were making parts of Asia better off than ever. Huge underground oil supplies had brought wealth to countries bordering the Persian Gulf—a major oil exporting region.

Thriving factories and shipyards helped Japan recover quickly after World War II. And by 1990, profitable export industries were springing up elsewhere in Asia, particularly in China, India, and parts of Southeast Asia. South Korea, Malaysia, Thailand, and the Philippines all grew rapidly during the 1980s, and became known as "Economic Tigers." Such rapid industrial growth was not limited to the larger nations: Some smaller countries—the so-called Little Tigers of Hong Kong, Singapore, and Taiwan—were among the fastest growing economies in the world in the 1980s and 1990s.

THE PEOPLES OF ASIA

Asian peoples make up dozens of different ethnic groups set apart from one another by such things as language or religion. Major groups include the Chinese in East and Southeast Asia, the Hindus of India, and the Muslim Arabs of Southwest Asia.

Asians speak hundreds of languages and dialects. All Chinese share one writing system, yet millions speak Cantonese or another dialect instead of the official Chinese language, Northern Mandarin.

The main Asian religions are Hinduism in India; Buddhism in Tibet and much of Southeast Asia; and Islam in places as far apart as Turkey and Indonesia. Asia's Christians live largely in Russia and the Philippines. Judaism is important only in Israel, Shinto in Japan.

Above *More than 12 million people live crammed in Bombay, India, many of them in slums that have sprung up near modern buildings.*

A VAST POPULATION

More than half of all human beings live in Asia. By the early 1990s the continent contained well over three billion people. More than one billion lived in China, the world's most populous nation.

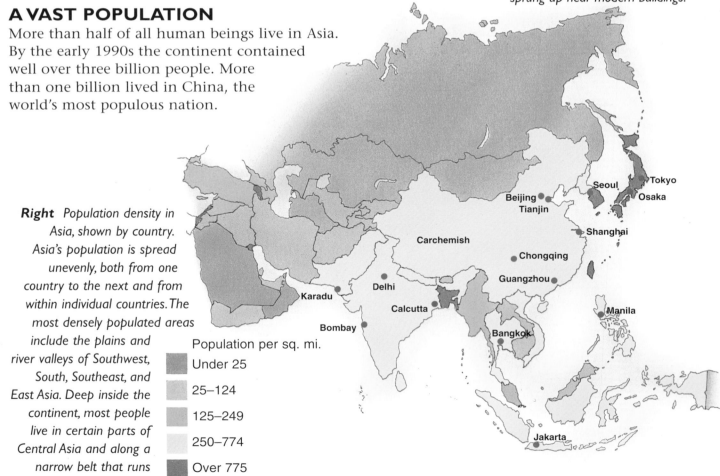

Right *Population density in Asia, shown by country. Asia's population is spread unevenly, both from one country to the next and from within individual countries. The most densely populated areas include the plains and river valleys of Southwest, South, Southeast, and East Asia. Deep inside the continent, most people live in certain parts of Central Asia and along a narrow belt that runs across Siberia.*

Population per sq. mi.

- Under 25
- 25–124
- 125–249
- 250–774
- Over 775
- Cities over 5 million

By 1995 there were more Chinese than there had been people in the whole world 150 years earlier. India ranked second, with roughly 940 million inhabitants, and it was fast catching up. In just five years India's numbers had risen by more than 115 million, equal to 40 percent of the entire population of the United States. For every hundred inhabitants, Pakistanis were multiplying at an even faster rate. But China's population growth had sharply slowed; the Chinese government had passed laws limiting family sizes to prevent China gaining more people than it could feed.

Asia's huge population is unevenly spread. Few people live in the great deserts of Southwest and Central Asia, on Tibet's chilly plateau, or in cold northern Siberia. But farming families teem on the fertile plains and hills around Asia's southwestern, southern, southeastern, and eastern rims—especially near the great Indus, Ganges, Huang Ho, and Yangtze rivers. Here, too, stand five of the world's ten largest cities, measured as continuously built-up areas. They are Tokyo with Yokohama, and Osaka with Kobe and Kyoto in Japan; Seoul in South Korea; and Bombay and Calcutta in India. By the mid-1990s each of these supercities held more than 11 million inhabitants.

Asian cities have grown rapidly as poor people have moved from countryside to town to find work. Their flimsy shacks sprawl around the rims of cities such as Bangkok in Thailand, Bombay and Delhi in India, and Manila in the Philippines.

To find better living conditions, many Asians have traveled much farther. Since 1970, millions have migrated from Southeast Asia to Europe and the United States and from Vietnam to other parts of Southeast Asia, Hong Kong, and Australia.

This mother and daughter fled from Vietnam to Hong Kong, where they were caught and kept in refugee camps. Many of their fellow refugees have been sent back to Vietnam.

LIVING STANDARDS

By Western standards most Asians are very poor. In the mid-1990s the average person in the United States earned roughly 10 times more than the average Russian, 70 times more than the average Chinese, and 85 times more than the average Indian. Worst off were the masses of poor Asian peasants scraping a meager living from the land. Best off were those working in factories and offices of countries with growing modern industries. Average income had risen sharply in Hong Kong, Singapore, Taiwan, South Korea, and some Chinese cities. In oil-rich Kuwait

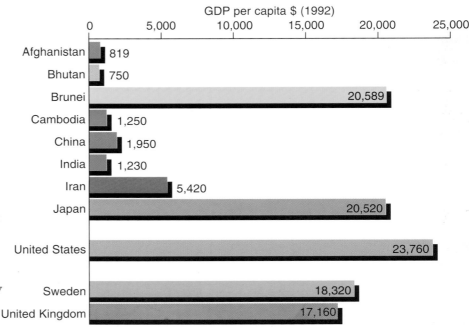

GDP per capita $ (1992)

Country	GDP per capita $ (1992)
Afghanistan	819
Bhutan	750
Brunei	20,589
Cambodia	1,250
China	1,950
India	1,230
Iran	5,420
Japan	20,520
United States	23,760
Sweden	18,320
United Kingdom	17,160

incomes nearly equaled those of the United States. In industrial Japan the average income was more than 25 percent higher than in the United States, and 75 percent higher than in Great Britain.

In much of Asia, low incomes mean poor living standards for most people, with inadequate food, housing, education, and medical help. Even so, most of the poorest countries have seen at least a few improvements.

New high-yielding kinds of rice have helped increase the amount of food that people eat in much of South, Southeast, and East Asia. The Chinese received nearly 50 percent more energy-providing food in the 1990s than 40 years before. But poor farmers, who depend mainly on the grains they grow for food, can suffer food-deficiency diseases. And if their main crop fails, some go hungry too. Famine followed the crop-destroying floods that struck Bangladesh in the mid-1980s.

Above   In this chart, the longer a bar the greater the wealth, or gross domestic product (GDP), of a person in the country named. GDP refers to all the economic activities that take place within a country.

Right   Families cook, eat, and sleep on this street. In Calcutta—India's largest city—thousands of people are so poor they live and die without homes of their own.

HOUSING, EDUCATION, AND HEALTH

Throughout Asia there are huge contrasts in the quality of housing. In Calcutta 100,000 homeless people sleep on the streets and six out of ten of Calcutta's citizens live crammed in flimsy shacks around the city's rim. But more prosperous Singapore has beaten overcrowding by knocking down its slums and rehousing people in 14 new towns containing altogether 700,000 apartments.

Asian education levels vary enormously, depending on each country's keenness and ability to pay for teachers, schools, and books. Half of all Indians and more than a quarter of all adult Chinese cannot read or write, yet illiteracy is less than one percent in Japan and countries of the former Soviet Union.

Doctors, modern hospitals, and medicines are scarce in much of the continent, yet Asian peoples are mostly healthier and longer lived than in 1950. Fewer starve, thanks largely to new heavy-cropping strains of food plants. Public health improvements have also played a major part. In developed areas, clean piped water and modern sewage systems mean that waterborne infections kill fewer people than they used to. Also, immunizing children against diseases such as poliomyelitis has saved many million lives. By the mid-1990s Chinese men could expect to live to 69—compared with 40 in 1955. In Japan the figure rose from 62 to 76—probably the highest in the world. At the other extreme, men could expect to live to only 43 in Afghanistan, a poor nation racked by civil war.

A couple admire stylish clothes in a store window at Shanghai's fanciest shopping center. Many Chinese now earn enough to buy expensive goods.

LIFE IN A *BUSTEE*

Gopal lives in Howrah, a poor part of Calcutta, India. His mother and father have five other children, and the whole family shares a tiny, one-roomed bustee—a flimsy house with a mud floor, wattle walls, and a corrugated iron roof. Everyone eats and sleeps in the same room, but Gopal's mother manages to keep it neat and the floor swept clean. Their street is a narrow alley packed with bustees. When it rains, water trickles in through holes, and any family that can't pay its rent gets thrown out by the landlord. In Calcutta one person in three lives in a home like Gopal's.

DEMOCRACY, MONARCHY, AND REVOLUTION

India, Israel, and Japan are three Asian nations that have long had democratic governments elected by their people. Other Asian nations with similar Western-style governments include Bangladesh, Malaysia, Pakistan, the Philippines, Singapore, and Taiwan. When the communist Soviet Union broke up to form new countries in 1991, Russia and the rest also held Western-type democratic elections to choose their new governments.

In some Asian nations people are less free to choose their own rulers. Royal families control Muslim Arab countries on the Persian Gulf: The king of Saudi Arabia, the emir of Kuwait, and the sultan of Oman all inherited their powers from their fathers.

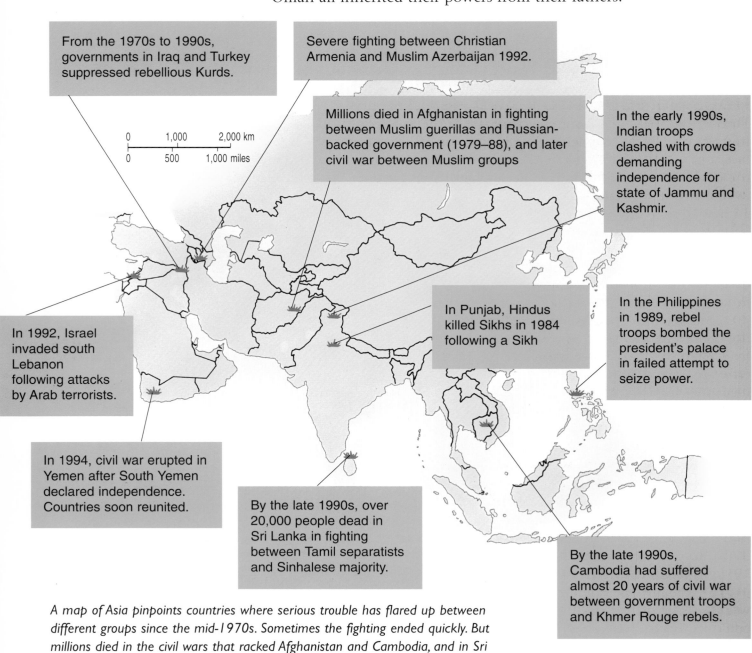

From the 1970s to 1990s, governments in Iraq and Turkey suppressed rebellious Kurds.

Severe fighting between Christian Armenia and Muslim Azerbaijan 1992.

Millions died in Afghanistan in fighting between Muslim guerillas and Russian-backed government (1979–88), and later civil war between Muslim groups

In the early 1990s, Indian troops clashed with crowds demanding independence for state of Jammu and Kashmir.

In 1992, Israel invaded south Lebanon following attacks by Arab terrorists.

In Punjab, Hindus killed Sikhs in 1984 following a Sikh

In the Philippines in 1989, rebel troops bombed the president's palace in failed attempt to seize power.

In 1994, civil war erupted in Yemen after South Yemen declared independence. Countries soon reunited.

By the late 1990s, over 20,000 people dead in Sri Lanka in fighting between Tamil separatists and Sinhalese majority.

By the late 1990s, Cambodia had suffered almost 20 years of civil war between government troops and Khmer Rouge rebels.

A map of Asia pinpoints countries where serious trouble has flared up between different groups since the mid-1970s. Sometimes the fighting ended quickly. But millions died in the civil wars that racked Afghanistan and Cambodia, and in Sri Lanka tens of thousands perished in fighting that has dragged on for years.

Left These Jewish settlers stand in line to vote in the Israeli general election of 1996. They are in the Arab town of Hebron, on the West Bank.

In 1979 Iran became unique as a country run by religious leaders, called ayatollahs. They came to power through an Islamic revolution in which the ruling royal family was overthrown. Once in power, the ayatollahs introduced strict Islamic laws enforced by harsh punishments, as decreed by Muhammad in the Koran. This movement, known as Islamic fundamentalism, is a growing threat to some governments in Southwest Asia, including Jordan, Saudi Arabia, and the United Arab Emirates and in Central Asian states such as Uzbekistan and Tajikistan.

Below Myanmar's military rulers refused to hand power to Aung San Suu Kyi after she won her country's first free election in years. Here she speaks to supporters outside her home, where she is being kept under house arrest.

MILITARY GOVERNMENTS

At one time or another, military leaders have run countries, including Burma (Myanmar), Indonesia, Iraq, Taiwan, Thailand, and Turkey. In 1990 Myanmar's army chiefs refused to hand over power to the country's first government to be fairly elected for 30 years and imprisoned political opponents.

Army leaders have often seized power to crush unrest. A number of Asian countries suffer unrest because they contain groups who hate one another. In several countries a small ethnic group fights or commits terrorist acts to try to win independence from a larger group ruling the country they both share. Kurds have stirred up trouble in Turkey and Iraq. Tamils have fought a long guerilla war in Sri Lanka. Palestinian terrorists shoot and bomb Jews in Israel. And in the Indian state of Jammu and Kashmir, Muslims of the Free Kashmir Movement resist Indian rule.

Trouble often involves strong differences of religion, for instance, between Muslims and Jews in Israel; Sunni and Shiite Muslims in Iraq; Hindus and Muslims in India; India's Hindus and Pakistan's Muslims; and Armenia's Christians and the Muslims of Azerbaijan.

RESOURCES, INDUSTRY, AND TRADE

About 60 out of every 100 Asians live by growing crops or raising livestock, compared with fewer than 5 out of 100 in parts of the Western World. Southwest Asia produces olives, grapes, wheat, and other Mediterranean crops, but the most productive farms lie in the moist lowlands of South, Southeast, and East Asia.

FARMING AND FOOD

Asian farms vary enormously in size. In parts of India and southern China, food grown on a very small plot feeds a whole family with rice, thanks to warm, moist soil producing several crops a year. Much larger farms include plantations growing crops to sell, for instance cotton in Central Asia, tea in India and Sri Lanka, and rubber in Indonesia, Malaysia, and Thailand. Some of the world's largest farms are the collective grain farms that sprang up in the former Soviet Union—many as big as some small countries. Here people worked for wages paid by the government. Communist China also set up big farms run by government officials. China's harvests rose sharply after 1979 when the Chinese government began encouraging farm workers to grow extra crops to sell for themselves.

Plans to bring water to parched fields help people cultivate some of the drier parts of Asia, but much of North, Central, and Southwest Asia remain too dry or cold for crops. Instead, herdsmen graze reindeer in the far north, yaks on the Tibetan Plateau, and camels, goats, sheep, and horses in much of Southwest and Central Asia. The animals provide milk, meat, butter, and cheese for food and hides and hair for tents and clothes.

Asia's croplands and rangelands produce a great deal of the world's chief foods and farm animals. China turns out more rice, wheat, eggs, horses, and pigs than any other nation, and India is first for bananas, millet, sugar, tea, cattle, and goats.

Left *By terracing and flooding slopes, Asian farmers learned long ago to produce rice crops on mountainsides as steep as these in Yunnan province, China.*

FORESTRY

Asian forests provide much of the world's wood, used for building, papermaking, or fuel. In North Asia the largest coniferous forest on Earth makes Russia the world's second largest softwood producer. Farther south, the tropical forests of India and Indonesia are among the world's chief sources of hardwoods.

FISHING

Millions of Asians live by fishing, and fish provide more than 25 percent of all animal protein eaten in Asia. More fish comes from the northwest Pacific than any other ocean. China and Japan rank first and second among the world's chief fish-catching nations, and Russia, India, Indonesia, Thailand, and South Korea are also in the top ten. Besides hunting for wild fish in seas and rivers, Asian people farm fish, shrimps, oysters, and edible seaweed in the coastal waters of East and Southeast Asia. In ponds and flooded rice fields Asians also raise freshwater fish, particularly carp. Asia produces 80 percent of the world's farmed fish. Chinese ponds alone yield more than half the world supply.

Above Men cutting tree trunks into logs in northern Russia. The vast forests in this region provide work and produce much valuable lumber.

Below The main fisheries of Asia's coast

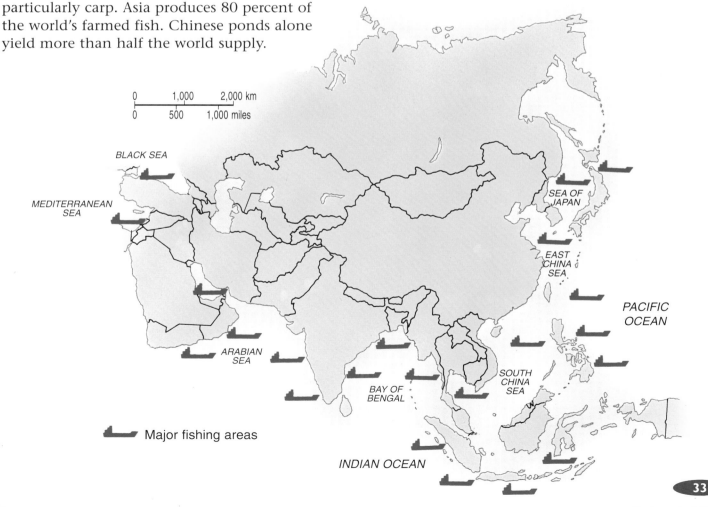

BLACK SEA

MEDITERRANEAN SEA

SEA OF JAPAN

EAST CHINA SEA

PACIFIC OCEAN

ARABIAN SEA

BAY OF BENGAL

SOUTH CHINA SEA

INDIAN OCEAN

Major fishing areas

MINERAL RESOURCES

The world's largest continent is also one of the richest in mineral reserves. For several minerals, China or else Russia—or another country of the former Soviet Union—ranks as the world leader. By the mid-1990s China was producing more iron ore and tin ore than any other nation. Countries of the former Soviet Union ranked high in copper ore, diamonds, phosphates, and lead ore. Malaysia ranked second for tin, and Kazakhstan and India came first and third in the world for chromium.

Some of the most striking production figures came from China, where output had risen sharply for export and to supply its fast-growing factories with raw materials. By 1993, China was producing almost 70 percent more salt, nearly three times as much tin ore, more than four times as much zinc ore, and seven times as much iron ore than it had just 13 years earlier.

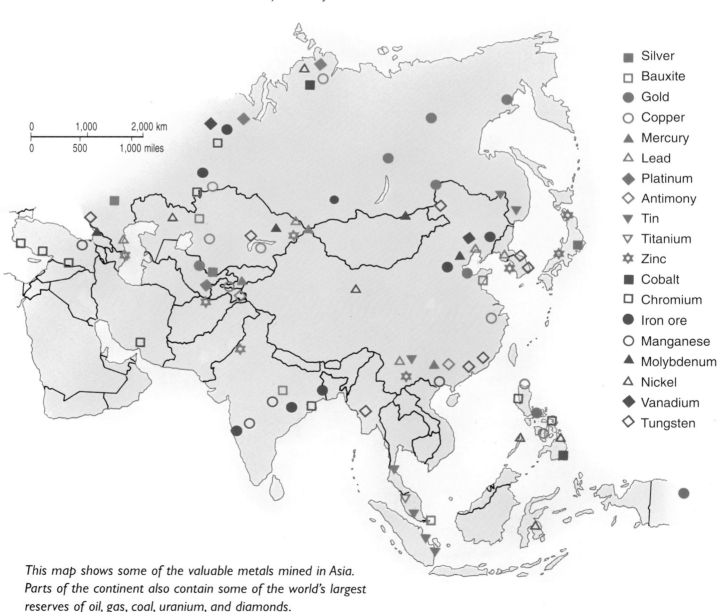

■	Silver
□	Bauxite
●	Gold
○	Copper
▲	Mercury
△	Lead
◆	Platinum
◇	Antimony
▼	Tin
▽	Titanium
✿	Zinc
■	Cobalt
□	Chromium
●	Iron ore
○	Manganese
▲	Molybdenum
△	Nickel
◆	Vanadium
◇	Tungsten

This map shows some of the valuable metals mined in Asia. Parts of the continent also contain some of the world's largest reserves of oil, gas, coal, uranium, and diamonds.

ENERGY SUPPLIES

Parts of Asia also have vast underground stocks of fossil fuels and the radioactive element uranium. Coal, oil, natural gas, and uranium fuel Asian power stations or are piped or shipped abroad. China is the world's top coal producer; India ranks third and Russia fourth. In oil-rich Southwest Asia, Saudi Arabia produces more oil than any other country. Russia and Indonesia are among the world's top four for natural gas. Kazakhstan and Uzbekistan rank third and fourth for uranium.

As the 20th century ended, water power contributed considerably to some countries' supplies of energy. Several nations were building huge dams to pen back river water for controlled release through turbines that generate electric current. In 1994 Vietnam's Hoa Binh Dam became fully operational, supplying nearly half the country's electricity. The same year, China began work on the world's two biggest-ever hydroelectric plants: the Longtan Power Station and the even-larger Three Gorges project. The Three Gorges Dam across the Yangtze River is designed to hold back a lake 375 miles long and produce 50 percent more electricity than the world's largest hydroelectric dam, in Paraguay, South America.

For millions of poor villagers in India and other parts of tropical Asia, burning fuelwood remains the chief way of heating homes and cooking food. Most of the trees cut down in South, Southeast, and East Asia end up in flames and smoke.

USING SMALL-SCALE WATER POWER

Small, cheap machines that use the energy in running water are making life much easier for women in some isolated mountain villages of Nepal. In 15 minutes one of these water turbines grinds as much grain into flour as a woman could in four hours by hand. Small water turbines can also generate electric current for lighting homes and heating electric stoves. This saves the women long hours spent collecting wood or paraffin to burn. It also means that people chop down fewer trees, so more remain, preventing rain washing away unprotected soil.

A Saudi Arabian oil refinery at dusk. Saudi Arabia is the world's largest oil producer, and the country's wealth is based almost entirely on the money it earns by selling its oil.

MANUFACTURING AND INDUSTRIAL DEVELOPMENT

By the mid-20th century Asia's industrial development lagged far behind that of the Western World. In the Soviet Union, heavy industries had sprung up along the Trans-Siberian Railroad, but Western peoples thought of the Chinese and Japanese as makers of cheap, poor copies of Western goods. Today, nations of the Pacific Ocean's rim have worldwide reputations as manufacturers of advanced products from cars to computer chips.

The industrial growth of East, Southeast, and South Asia began with hardworking Asian peoples who were paid low wages to produce goods far more cheaply than Western factories could make them. Almost equally important have been Asian governments' programs offering benefits to companies that invest cash and skill to build new factories equipped with modern machinery. The results have been to make the Asian Pacific region's young industrial economies among the fastest growing in the world.

THE GROWTH OF JAPAN

In the dash for growth, Japan led the way, and by the 1970s it was a major producer of chemicals, ships, and steel. Computer-controlled processes then helped new Japanese factories to mass produce high-quality cameras, cars, and computer chips. In the early 1990s, Japan was the world's biggest producer of steel, cars, and ships and the second largest producer of zinc, cement, synthetic rubber, and tires. The Japanese are now also among the world leaders in biotechnology and data processing.

By the 1980s Hong Kong, Singapore, South Korea, and Taiwan—the so-called little tigers—had followed Japan's lead and were developing modern industries as well. Now, industrialization is taking off in mainland China, India, Indonesia, Malaysia, the Philippines, and Thailand. By the early 1990s China led the world in tin and zinc refining and making cement and televisions and came second in steel and radio production.

A worker puts finishing touches to a family car in a Japanese factory. Japanese carmakers have become world famous for innovation, reliability, and high productivity.

Above *Each year, millions of tourists visit Bangkok, the capital of Thailand, to marvel at the city's ornate Buddhist shrines and temples.*

Meanwhile Asian service industries (businesses supplying services, not manufactured goods) expanded. By 1990 Japan's Dai-Ichi Kangyo Bank was the world's biggest commercial bank, the State Bank of India had more branches than any other bank, and Singapore and Tokyo had become great financial centers. Tourism was also growing fast. More Asians than ever began traveling around their continent, and cheap long-haul flights brought record numbers of Americans and Europeans to cities such as Jerusalem, Bangkok, Beijing, Samarkand, Singapore, Hong Kong, and Tokyo and to such famous Asian landmarks as the Taj Mahal in India and Indonesia's idyllic island, Bali.

WHERE CITIES SPROUT

Since 1979 China's communist government has created special economic zones (see map below) and open cities where foreign investors can set up low-cost, high-tech factories, and run them cheaply. The results have been spectacular and nowhere more so than in Shenzhen. In 1980 this small town grew food for the nearby British colony of Hong Kong. When Shenzhen became a special economic zone, new factories sprang up producing electrical goods, electronic components, clothes, drinks, and plastics. Employers paid five times the Chinese average wage, so workers flooded in. In fewer than 15 years, Shenzhen's population exploded from 30,000 to 3,000,000.

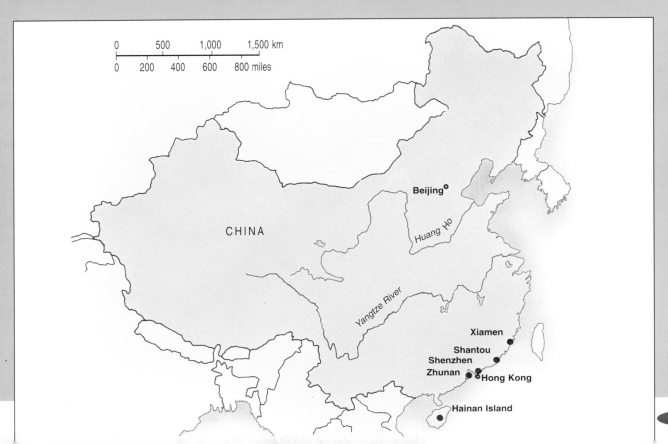

TRANSPORTATION LINKS

Much of mainland Asia lacks the well-developed transportation systems of the West, and high mountains make land transportation difficult between North and South Asia.

Surfaced roads link inland cities to one another and the chief ports. In richer countries such as Japan, Israel, and Arab nations on the Persian Gulf, cars, trucks, and buses move people and goods along smooth paved roads. But Asia's country roads are still mostly unsurfaced. Villagers mainly walk or cycle and carry loads or move them by cart, often with the help of donkeys, camels, or oxen. People, animals, bicycles, cars, and trucks jostle one another in the teeming streets of such cities as Bombay.

Above Roads that are often washed away by floods make cross-country travel difficult on Sulawasi, a large island forming part of Indonesia.

Few Asian nations have good railroads, but Japan's railroad system is extremely modern, India has a well-developed network, and Russia's Trans-Siberian Railroad through North Asia is the longest railroad line on Earth.

Air traffic has grown enormously to many parts of Asia and especially to Hong Kong and Japan. In both, lack of space on land has meant building airports on artificial islands. In the 1990s Hong Kong's Chek Lap Kok Airport became the biggest civil engineering project in the world.

In China and much of South and Southeast Asia, rivers form important highways traveled by craft, including barges, junks, and sampans. The Mediterranean Sea, Indian Ocean, and Pacific Ocean provide sea routes for oil tankers and other cargo ships linking Asian ports with one another and the rest of the world. By the mid-1990s, Singapore had become the world's busiest container port. Three hundred cargo ships sail in and out each day, loading or unloading goods packed in thousands of containers as big as buses.

Right Giant cranes unload bus-sized containers from a ship at Singapore. Offshore, other vessels wait their turn to drop or pick up cargo. The port of Singapore can handle hundreds of ships every day.

IMPORTS AND EXPORTS

As Asian nations industrialize, countries like Japan import huge quantities of iron ore, lead, oil, wool, and cotton to supply their factories with energy and raw materials. Asian exports include fossil fuels and raw materials, especially lumber from Southeast Asia, natural gas from Russia, and oil from Southwest Asia. From East and Southeast Asian factories, cars, motorcycles, cameras, hi-fis, televisions, video recorders, computers, and computer software are sold around the world. Western countries that used to make these goods now buy them largely from Japan, South Korea, Taiwan, and other Asian countries, because their products are often better and cheaper than those made in the West.

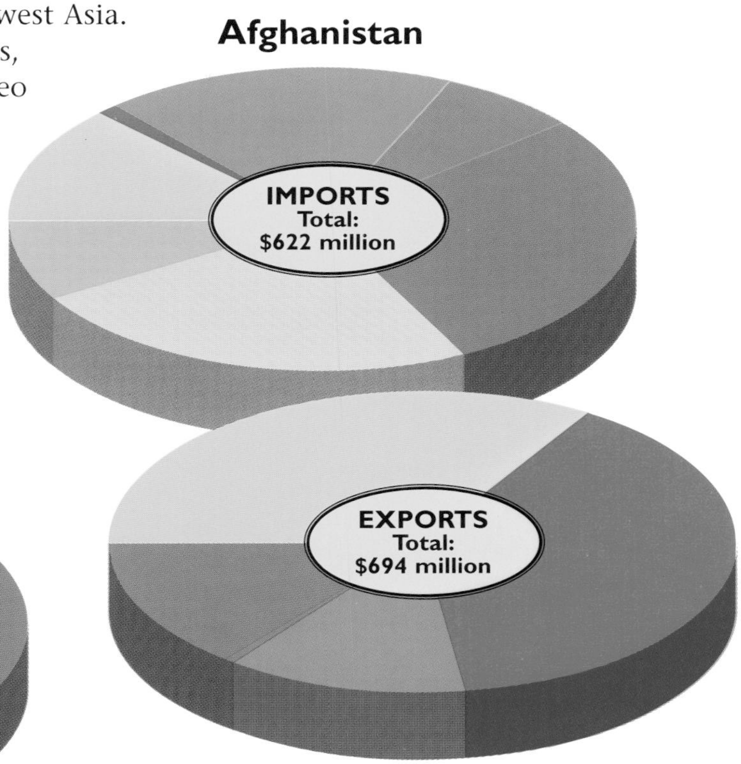

Afghanistan

IMPORTS
Total:
$622 million

EXPORTS
Total:
$694 million

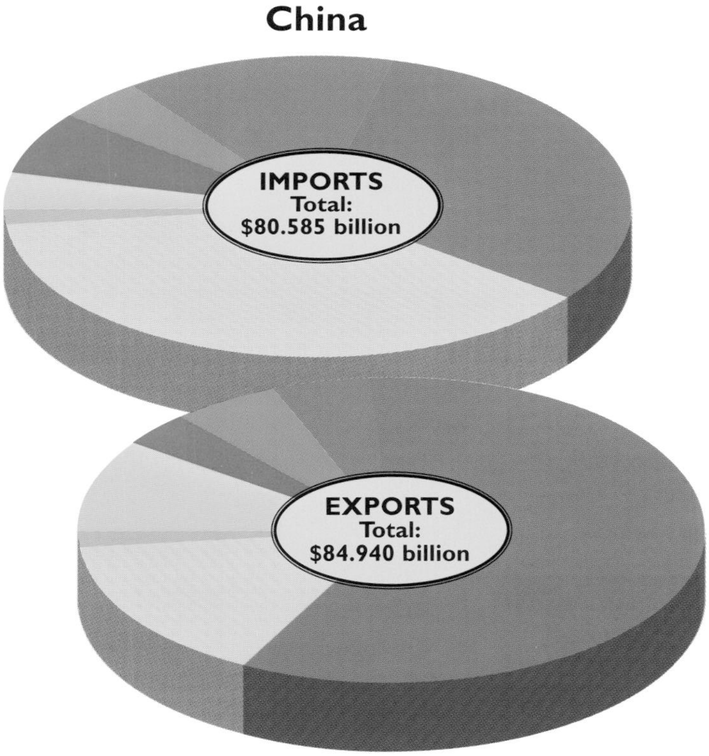

China

IMPORTS
Total:
$80.585 billion

EXPORTS
Total:
$84.940 billion

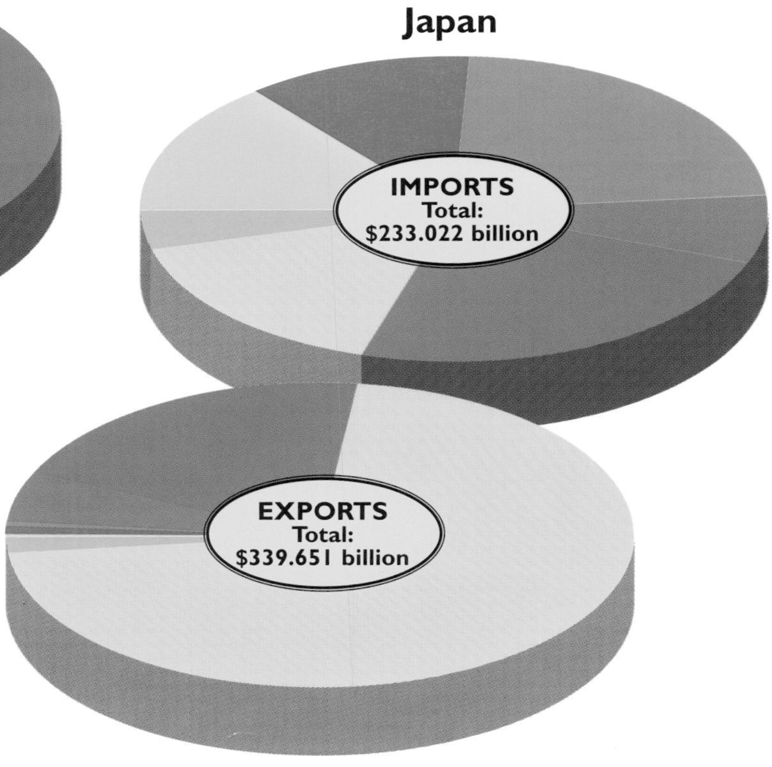

Japan

IMPORTS
Total:
$233.022 billion

EXPORTS
Total:
$339.651 billion

KEY TO PIE CHARTS

- Food and live animals
- Crude materials (inedible) excluding fuels
- Mineral fuels, lubricants, and related materials
- Chemicals
- Manufactured goods
- Machinery and transportation equipment
- Other

THE ENVIRONMENT

Asia's multiplying population has a growing need for living space, food, fuel, and raw materials. Extra people also produce extra waste. These changes are harming both the environment and the people, who depend upon it.

ENVIRONMENT AND DEVELOPMENT

In tropical Asia most good, level land is already being farmed, so people chop down forests on steep slopes to make new fields. They also cut down trees for fuel and lumber. Southeast Asia's once-vast rain forests could soon be just a memory. Where tree roots no longer hold the soil together, heavy tropical rain races downhill, washing away soil and flooding valleys. Floods and soil erosion are badly damaging much land.

As people destroy forests, forest creatures lose their homes and become scarcer. China's giant panda is already rare, and there are far fewer Asian elephants than there were in 1950. Tigers are at special risk from being killed by poachers who sell their bones for use in Chinese medicines.

Low coasts and their wildlife have suffered heavily in South and Southeast Asia, where people clear mangrove forests and quarry coral for cement. Without coral reefs or mangrove forests to protect low shores, waves are wearing away these coasts.

Now, too, Asian fishermen are catching sea fish faster than they breed. Between 1989 and 1992 the northwest Pacific catch fell by 10 percent. Desperate to increase their catch, some fishermen poison coral reefs with cyanide. This kills not just fish but all other reef life.

Waste harms the environment differently, especially its seas. Most Asian coastal waters have suffered from the poisonous effects of city sewage; factory waste; soil, pesticides, and fertilizers washed off farms; or oil spilled by ships. As the Caspian Sea mysteriously rises, pools of oil and chemical and radioactive wastes dumped around its rim seep in, threatening its seals and fish.

Environmental damage hits humans, too. Forest peoples lose their homes and their way of life as lumber companies cut down Borneo's rain forests. In Siberian cities, thousands of people suffer ill-health caused by smoke and fumes belching from old-fashioned factories.

Below *A worker carries coral taken from a Sri Lankan coral reef. The coral will be heated in a lime kiln to turn it into cement.*

Some Asian countries have attempted to repair the damage. For instance, in the 1970s Indian villagers began chaining themselves to trees to keep them from being felled. Later China, India, and South Korea began replanting forests. The World Bank and the United Nations helped launch the Tropical Forestry Action Plan supposed to safeguard tropical forests. In 1983 the United Nations also launched a Regional Mangrove Project to save mangrove forests in Asia and the Pacific area. The United Nations Environment Program has produced plans to clean up polluted seas worldwide, and in 1995 a World Bank report urged people to farm more fish to make up for falling catches of fish caught at sea. Unfortunately, most Asian countries are still too poor to pay to correct the situation.

Above *The rising Caspian Sea floods low-lying oil fields and their electrical installations.*

INVISIBLE DEATH

One night in 1984, 45 tons of a gas used for making pesticide leaked silently from an American-owned factory in the Indian city of Bhopal. Wind gently wafted poisonous fumes from the Union Carbide Corporation's factory across the closely packed homes of poor people living crammed into that part of Bhopal. Scores died in their sleep. Others developed serious eye troubles or breathing difficulties. Children and old people suffered most. Altogether the gas killed more than 3,300 victims and affected 100,000, while 220,000 terrified survivors fled. The Bhopal disaster was the world's worst-ever industrial accident.

THE FUTURE

Population growth will slow down in the 21st century, but by 2025 Asia could have more than 4.5 billion people—roughly one billion more than in 2000, and as many as the whole world held in 1980. By 2050 Pakistan might overtake Russia and the United States to become the world's third most populous country. As traffic clogs the biggest cities, people could move out, forming smaller cities in between. A "corridor" of cities linked by roads and tunnels might stretch 1,250 miles from Beijing in China through Korea to Tokyo in Japan.

BOOMING ECONOMIES

Fast-growing economies will expand still more. In 1995 ASEAN (the Association of South-East Asian Nations) gained its seventh trading partner, Vietnam, and the NICs (newly industrialized countries) of East and Southeast Asia seemed set to boost their share of world trade. The economies of China, Malaysia, and Thailand should grow especially fast. When Hong Kong is returned to China in 1997, China could become the world's leading economy by 2020.

Cars, vans, taxis, bikes, and colorful buses form a traffic jam in Karachi, the largest and fastest-growing city in Pakistan.

CONFLICT AHEAD?

In the future, the Chinese might find it harder to feed themselves. By 1995 the world's largest wheat producer was running short of grain. By 2020 China might have to buy 10 percent of its grain from abroad. Food shortages or other problems could unsettle some major countries. Chinese peasants envy the new wealth of China's cities, and in Russia millions became worse off after the Soviet Union broke up. In both countries, discontented people could cause trouble for their governments. In Muslim countries of Southwest Asia more conflict seems likely, between those wanting to modernize on Western lines and Muslims insisting that everyone obeys strict Islamic laws. In Israel, Muslim terrorists could go on killing Jews.

Despite trade agreements, trade wars—in which nations block or limit imports of each other's goods—might break out with the Americans on one side and the Chinese or Japanese on the other. Old disagreements between nations might even spark off real wars. Likely troublemakers include Iraq, North Korea, and communist China, which wants to seize the non-communist Chinese island of Taiwan. Some people also fear that a Russian leader might one day fight to win back countries that once belonged to the Soviet Union.

Economic growth will affect Asia's natural environment deeply. Forests will continue to shrink to make way for farms, roads, and reservoirs. As rare forest creatures lose their homes, some could disappear forever. At sea, unless Asian fishermen reduce their catch, fish stocks will go on shrinking, too. But at least those Asian nations with growing economies and rising incomes should be able to afford to do more to curb pollution.

These Chinese villagers lead far poorer lives than many Chinese city dwellers. Resentful country folk might one day rise against their government, which has helped to make the cities rich but left rural populations poor.

TIME LINE

B.C.

1,800,000 *Homo erectus* appears in Asia for the first time. *Homo erectus* is followed by *Homo sapiens neanderthalensis*, then around 100,000 B.C. *Homo sapiens sapiens* (modern humans) appeared.

30,000 Asian peoples enter Europe from Southwest Asia. They have probably already spread through Asia to Australia. Later, Asians also populate North and South America, when a land bridge links northern Asia with the northern tip of North America.

10,000–9,000 Slash-and-burn agriculture is being practiced in Thailand and Taiwan.

8,500–7,000 Middle Eastern people (in what are now Iraq, Iran, Afghanistan, and Turkey) begin to swap hunting and gathering for a farming and herding way of life.

3,500–3,000 Early civilizations using writing develop in the Tigris-Euphrates river valleys.

2,500 Cultivation of millet, buckwheat, beans, and probably rice is common throughout East and Southeast Asia at this time.

2,500 Civilizations spring up in the Indus Valley and in northern Syria. South Chinese and Southeast Asians develop maritime skills, trading by sea as far west as Bengal.

1766–1122 China's cities begin to grow more important under the Shang, or Yin, dynasty.

1700 Indo-Europeans, themselves the descendants of an ancient Asian migration, invade India, using horses. They also destroy the civilization of the Indus Valley.

1122–221 Chou dynasty replaces Shang in China. The Chou dynasty begins many of the cultural practices still found in China today.

330 Alexander the Great conquers the Persian Empire from the west. His armies smash through Afghanistan, into Central Asia, and down into the Punjab.

A.D.

7th century Islamic religion rises and spreads from Southwest Asia.

13th century Genghis Khan and his successors unite most of Asia under their control, ruling China, Central Asia, much of Southwest Asia, and some parts of Eastern Europe.

15th century Muslim forces from what is now Turkey destroy the remnants of the Byzantine Empire and establish an Asian/European kingdom that will survive into the 20th century. This kingdom ends only with the breakup of the Ottoman Empire at the end of World War I in 1918.

19th century Asian imperialism gives way to European imperialism, as European powers begin to expand into Asia. Russia expands through Central Asia and all the way to the Pacific. The British control India; the French move into Indochina; the Dutch occupy the East Indies; and Spain rules the Philippines until 1898, when the U.S. purchases them for $200 million. Of the Asian nations, only Japan shows expansionist tendencies, through a growing influence in Korea and China during the 19th and 20th centuries.

1939–1945 World War II: Only the later years of the war (from the end of 1941 onward) are fought in Asia. Japan threatens British India, removing the French from Indochina and heading out across the Pacific toward Hawaii and Australia. Japan is eventually beaten by Allied forces, finally being forced to surrender in 1945 when atomic bombs are dropped on the cities of Hiroshima and Nagasaki.

1945 onward European imperialism begins to die out in Asia as former colonies gain their independence (see map p. 24). However, Asia divides along communist and capitalist lines during the cold war (1950–1989). During the Korean War (1950–53) and the Vietnam War (1957–75), the cold war becomes "hot," as Communist forces backed by China fight capitalist forces backed by the U.S. and other Western powers.

1949 The Communist People's Republic of China is declared in Peking by Mao Zedong ("Chairman Mao"). His non-communist rivals move to the island of Taiwan.

1950 The Korean War sparks a manufacturing boom in Japan, as UN forces require materials for the war, and the United States decides to encourage Japanese industry to prevent the spread of communism.

1952 U.S. occupation of Japan ends.

1970s Japan develops the world's most powerful economy.

1979 The Shah (hereditary ruler) of Iran is forced to flee by revolutionary forces. An extremist Islamic government, led by Ayatollah Khomeini, takes power. The event marks the increase of Islamic fundamentalism in Asia— soon there are fundamentalist movements throughout Southwest Asia and other regions, including the Middle East, Pakistan, India, Indonesia, and large parts of the former USSR.

1980s Japanese banks, businesses, and manufacturers expand throughout the globe.

1980s Economic Tigers begin to emerge around the Pacific Rim: South Korea, Malaysia, and, to a lesser extent, Taiwan, Thailand, and the Philippines. China abandons hard-line communism and begins to encourage the expansion of trade, announcing the creation of its Special Economic Zones.

1989 onward The breakup of the USSR, following the collapse of communism there and in Eastern Europe, affects much of northern and Central Asia. The USSR divides into separate countries with their own governments. Many are Islamic states.

1997 Hong Kong is returned to China after 99 years of British government.

GLOSSARY

Arctic The region within and bordering the Arctic Circle.

Biotechnology Biological science put to work to make new useful substances or organisms.

Bronze Age A time when people used bronze tools and weapons. In Asia it followed the New Stone Age.

Communist government A type of government that largely controls who owns what in its country and how its people live, work, and think.

Data processing Using computers in business.

Delta An apron of lowland built of sediments dumped by a river into a sea or lake.

Democratic government A government chosen by and for the people, who may vote for any political party they please.

Desert An area in which the annual precipitation (rain or snow) is less than 8 inches.

Earthquake A shaking of the earth's crust, often where one of the earth's plate moves suddenly against another.

Economy A country's economy involves its goods and services, trade, and the income of its people.

Ethnic A group sharing a language, a religion, customs, or something else that sets it apart from other groups.

Export To sell abroad.

Food-deficiency disease A disease caused by getting too little of some kind of nourishment.

Hardwood Wood obtained from oak, teak, and other broadleaf trees.

Heavy industry A type of industry producing basic manufactured goods, for instance, iron and steel.

Hunter-gatherer Someone who depends on hunting wild animals and gathering wild plants for food.

Hydroelectricity Electricity produced from the energy in falling water.

Illiteracy Inability to read and write.

Immunizing Giving injections or pills that protect against certain infectious diseases.

Import To buy from abroad.

Industrial Revolution The cheap mass production of goods by machines that began in Europe in the 18th century.

Iron Age A time when people used iron for making tools and weapons. It followed the Bronze Age.

Junk A wooden Chinese sailing boat.

Life expectancy How long a group of people can expect to live.

Living standard The goods and services that people can afford to buy. The more they can afford, the higher their living standard.

Mangrove A type of tree that grows on low, muddy shores in tropical countries.

Mineral A useful substance obtained from the ground, for instance, iron ore. Scientists use "mineral" for substances made of only certain types of chemicals.

New Stone Age A time when people had learned to farm but not to make metal tools.

Old Stone Age A time when people lived as hunter-gatherers, using tools and weapons of stone and wood.

Ore Any mineral found in the ground and containing a useful substance such as iron or tin.

Pacific Rim The lands around the Pacific Ocean.

Permafrost A layer of permanently frozen ground below the surface.

Plate One of the rigid slabs forming the earth's crust. Its full name is tectonic plate.

Plateau An area of flattish highland.

Protein A type of food needed to build and repair the body. Protein foods include meat and milk.

Public health Work done to keep a community of people healthy, for instance, immunization and providing clean drinking water.

Rangeland Land used for grazing domesticated animals, particularly cattle, goats, or sheep.

Raw materials Substances used in the production of manufactured goods.

Sampan a flat-bottomed Chinese boat with oars.

Sediments Particles of sand, silt, or mud that settle on the bottom of a sea, lake, or river valley.

Service industry An industry providing services such as tourism, banking, or insurance.

Shiite A member of the Shia Muslim sect.

Softwood Wood from coniferous trees.

Steppe A grassy, treeless plain.

Sunni A member of the Sunni Muslim sect.

Taiga The coniferous forest of Siberia.

Tundra The cold, treeless plain lying mainly north of the Arctic Circle.

Western In geography, relating to the Western World: chiefly North America and Europe.

World Bank An international bank set up by the United Nations to lend money to governments. Its full name is the International Bank for Reconstruction and Development.

FURTHER INFORMATION

Organizations to Contact

You can obtain information on many of the countries presented in this book at their embassies in Washington D.C. The addresses for several of them appear below.

People's Republic of China
2300 Connecticut Avenue, NW
Washington, D.C. 20008

India
2107 Massachusetts Avenue, NW
Washington, D.C. 20008

Japan
2520 Massachuesetts Avenue, NW
Washinton, D.C. 20008

Books to Read

Brill, Marlene T. *Mongolia*. Enchantment of the World. Danbury, CT: Children's Press, 1992.

Civilizations of Asia. History of the World. Austin, TX: Raintree Steck-Vaughn, 1988.

Coblence, Jean-Michel. *Asian Civilizations*. Human Story. Morristown, NJ: Silver Burdett Press, 1988.

Conklin, Paul. *Land of Yesterday, Land of Tomorrow: Discovering Chinese Central Asia*. New York: Dutton Children's Books, 1994.

Ganeri, Anita. *Southeast Asia*. Places and People. Danbury, CT: Franklin Watts, 1995.

Lerner Geography Department Staff, ed. *Cyprus in Pictures*. Visual Geography. Minneapolis, MN: Lerner Group, 1992.

Mason, Antony. *Southeast Asia*. World in View. Austin, TX: Raintree Steck-Vaughn, 1992.

Rigg, Jonathan. *Southeast Asia*. Country Fact Files. Austin, TX: Raintree Steck-Vaughn, 1995.

Solberg, S.E. *The Land & People of Korea*. Portraits of the Nations. New York: HarperCollins Children's Books, 1991.

Srinivasan, Rodbika. *India*. Cultures of the World. Tarrytown, NY: Marshall Cavendish, 1991.

Thomas, Paul. *The Central Asian States*. Former Soviet States. Brookfield, CT: Millbrook Press, 1992.

Waterlow, Julia. *China*. Economically Developing Countries. New York: Thomson Learning, 1995.

INDEX

The figures in **bold** refer to photographs

© Copyright 1997 Wayland (Publishers) Ltd.

Forbush Memorial Library
118 MAIN STREET P.O. BOX 468
WESTMINSTER, MA 01473-0468

	DATE DUE		